The

Art of Teaching

Also by Jay Parini

The

Art of Teaching

Jay Parini

OXFORD
UNIVERSITY PRESS
2005

OXFORD
UNIVERSITY PRESS

Oxford   New York
Auckland   Bangkok   Buenos Aires   Cape Town   Chennai
Dar es Salaam   Delhi   Hong Kong   Istanbul   Karachi   Kolkata
Kuala Lumpur   Madrid   Melbourne   Mexico City   Mumbai   Nairobi
São Paulo   Shanghai   Taipei   Tokyo   Toronto

Copyright © 2005 by Jay Parini

Published by Oxford University Press, Inc.
198 Madison Avenue, New York, New York 10016
www.oup.com

Oxford is a registered trademark of Oxford University Press

Library of Congress Cataloging-in-Publication Data
Parini, Jay.
The art of teaching / Jay Parini.
p. cm
ISBN-13: 978-0-19-516969-0

   Parini, Jay.
   1. College teachers—United States—Biography.
   2. College teaching—Vocational guidance.
I. Title.

LA2317. P335A3 2004
378. 1'2—dc22   2004005443

Book design: planettheo.com

Printed in the United States of America on acid-free paper

For Devon, the best teacher of all

Contents

Preface

Teaching is not only a job of work. A teacher is charged with waking students to the nature of reality, providing rigorous introduction to a certain discipline, and creating an awareness of their responsibility as citizens trained in the art of critical thinking. Of course most young people in the history of the world, even the brightest among them, have not been nurtured in this way. Education is expensive, and—unfortunately—this expense has been largely supported by states that want certain things taught and many things avoided. But education is never as much about the past as about the future. Indeed, Paolo Freire, a theorist of education, once reminded us that "to think of history as possibility is to recognize education as possibility. It is to recognize that if education cannot do everything, it can achieve some things."

In this book, I contemplate some of those things, meditating on the context in which they can be accomplished. After beginning with an autobiographical chapter about my own experience within the educational system, in the United States and Britain, I move on to contemplate aspects of the teaching life, including what one wears in the classroom, how one cultivates an individual teaching persona, and how one can manage to teach and continue to do writing and research at the same time. In a further section, I look closely at the nitty-gritty of teaching. I talk about lectures, seminars, and office hours: the basic teaching formats. I discuss the thorny matter of politics in relation to a teacher's larger responsibilities to society as well as to the student. In "Letter to a Young Teacher," I speak frankly to young teachers about the profession itself, its pitfalls and possibilities. I try to include in this "letter" the things I wish somebody had said to me at the start of my career.

I address all of the above issues from the viewpoint of a college teacher who has worked in the classroom for over 30 years. For the past decade or more, I have contributed occasional essays on aspects of teaching and the culture of education to the *Chronicle of Higher Education*. Many topics included here appeared in those pages, although I have taken into account further thoughts, reconsiderations, and further experience.

This is a book for anyone interested in higher education, although it will appeal especially to young teachers, those who must thread their way through the complex maze of the system. I suspect it will interest older teachers as well, although they will no doubt find much to disagree with. It is in the nature of things for teachers and scholars to disagree, and I welcome the discussions that may follow from this book.

Teaching is a challenging, exhilarating profession, as anyone will know who has stepped into a classroom, as if naked before a young, demanding audience, feeling the pressure of their gaze, the huge need in their hearts, and the material in their heads that needs shaping, realignment, and supplementation. Of course I'm deeply grateful to my students for allowing me to perform a crucial function in their lives. This book reflects my gratitude and my hopes for them as well. Whatever has been done, can be done better. That is my fundamental premise, in life and in these reflections.

The

Art of Teaching

Beginnings

Beginnings. One of the things I have most prized about working in the academy is the sense of beginnings. There is always a fresh start, with new students, new colleagues, new courses. Even old colleagues somehow look new in September, when the light of the sun seems especially bright, gearing up for a final summery blast before the inevitable decline, what Robert Frost in "The Oven Bird" called "that other fall we name the fall."

It has always seemed ironic to me that one begins anything in the fall, or that a sense of starting over should connect, visually, with the blood-bright failure of so much greenery. Emotionally, the school year ought to open in springtime, when the buds do: there would be a feeling in the air of everything starting over. But it doesn't work that way. Somewhere, long ago, somebody thought up the notion that academic terms should begin in the fall: probably when the work of harvesting was over, so that farm boys could study with impunity.

I often think of "Spring and Fall," a poem by Gerard Manley Hopkins. In it, the narrator happens upon a young girl, Margaret, who stands amid a typical autumn scene, with the golden leaves tumbling around her. For unknown reasons, she is weeping. The poet, more to himself than to the girl, concludes:

Ah! as the heart grows older
It will come to such sights colder
By and by, nor spare a sigh
Though worlds of wanwood leafmeal lie;
And yet you will weep and know why.
Now no matter, child, the name:
Sorrow's springs are the same.
Nor mouth had, no nor mind, expressed
What heart heard of, ghost guessed:
It is the blight man was born for,
It is Margaret you mourn for.

In other words, Margaret (like the narrator as well as the poem's readers) must go the way of all leaves, whether or not she consciously knows it. When we feel sorry in the autumn, we are mourning our own mutability.

On the other hand, the rhythm of the academic world runs counter to this natural grieving, so aptly symbolized by the seasons. According to the academic calendar, fall means starting over, springing into life again after the torpid drowse of summer. For me as a child, the beginning of the school year always meant a set of fresh clothes, new shoes, a packet of unsharpened pencils, and notebooks as yet unblemished by feeble attempts to write or cipher. Most crucially, it meant a new teacher: some unknown woman with the title of "Miss" (I never encountered a male teacher until junior high) whose voice pattern and idiosyncratic habits I would just have to accept, no matter how much I longed for last year's teacher. The new year also meant a set of unspoken rules I must discover the hard way, through experience.

Although—like every child—I hated to see the summer end, the beginning of school held out a sense of promise: a fresh chance at playing myself, with the live option to try on new personae—those brittle masks we mold to our skin, that eventually become indistinguishable from what we call the self, that many-faceted figuration we present to the world. There was also the chance to reinvent my relationship to the rest of the class: to make old friends new, to discover which classmates I might have overlooked or overestimated. It meant recalculating my place within the group, making adjustments and being adjusted by others. (The latter could be quite painful, and remains so.)

In 1960, I was myself able to make a rather dramatic switch of masks when moving from grade school to junior high: one of several crucial junctions in any student's life. I had been fiercely, almost pathologically, shy; indeed, wallflower didn't begin to describe my grade-school persona—I was the wall itself, *sans* petals. Over the summer, I stumbled onto a book in the town library: *How To Win Friends and Influence People* by Dale Carnegie. I read it over and over, then copied out Carnegie's rules for winning friends, taping them to my bedroom wall. I memorized them, and they still ring in my head four decades later. "Be hearty in your approbation and lavish in your praise," said Carnegie (I'm quoting from memory). That particular rule caught my attention.

When the school year started, I spent the first weeks in a blaze of observation. Carnegie claimed there was something worth praising in everyone, and I believed him. Deciding to be systematic about this, I wrote down the names of everyone in my homeroom class, seat by seat. Within a few weeks, I had found (and noted in my diary) something positive about every student in the room. Soon my attack began. "You have an amazing throwing arm," I said to Jack, whose talents with a baseball caught my attention one day after school. "You really ought to consider going out for the baseball team next spring." To Elaine: "When you pronounce words in Spanish class, you really sound, well, *Spanish*. Have you ever been to Spain?" It seemed there was something in everybody to relish: Ralph's jump shot on the basketball court, Sally's handwriting, Rosemary's way of asking useful questions in World History. If anybody saw through my campaign of hearty approbation, I'm still not aware of it.

What I was doing was *not*, I reassured myself, just naked flattery. I believed—damn it, I still do!—that everyone has something of value to offer, and that no harm is ever done by pointing this out to them. For me, the Carnegie approach worked wonders; that is, I established a beachhead of sorts within a projected, utterly strange, brave new world of selfhood. I had, in fact, started over as a human being. Good things naturally followed from this early, rather gauche, experiment in trying on a new mask. Mostly, I learned that it was possible to begin again, with very little, and that one is not necessarily stuck with an old mask if it fits uncomfortably.

Years later, I still find beginnings attractive for what they offer in the way of opportunities for change, although the first days and weeks of school are not without their small terrors and discomforts. Indeed, as I was writing this, I got an e-mail from a colleague saying that she hadn't taught in a while, and she was actually frightened of her students. I know the feeling: that dread, as one approaches class for the first time in September. It can be difficult to begin again, to invent everything from the ground up, to learn the names of the students, their foibles, their likes and dislikes. There is so much to absorb in a short time. It can make you dizzy with apprehension.

Teaching and writing have a lot in common here. "In creating," wrote James Russell Lowell in "A Fable for Critics," "the only hard thing's to begin." In the classroom, starting over can feel daunting.

Teaching—again, like writing—is a brave act of self-presentation, and with every new class, the need to reinvent oneself is vividly, even scarily, at hand. In fact, good teachers have no choice but to consider their public selves in a calculated fashion: a subject I address in detail later in this volume. The classroom is a form of theater, and the teacher must play various roles, often in an exaggerated manner: wise man, fool, tempter, comforter, coach, confessor. And that is just for starters. (One soon gets used to the fact that an element of artifice is involved in classroom performances. In fact, there is nothing *natural* about teaching; a good teacher may look natural, much as Michael Jordan always looked natural when he went up for a dunk or fell away from the basket, making an extraordinary shot. The natural look, however, is acquired, the product of endless practice.)

Despite the challenges of teaching, it is hard not to like having a job where you can start over every September, shredding the previous year's failures and tossing them out the window like so much confetti. It's not quite so simple, of course, especially in the years before one has tenure, when every black mark seems to smudge and cover the whole page of your copybook. Nevertheless, mistakes made in the previous year can (and must) be regarded as opportunities: one can always be better prepared this time around, smarter about the sequence of items on the syllabus, more patient with the various kinds of students one finds deeply annoying, more supportive and genuinely useful to those one can really help in concrete ways. One of the great boons of teaching is the sense of self-development, of improving as one matures. It's *always* possible to do a better job the next time around.

For me, it's academic New Year's Eve every September: a time for bold resolutions that I know I'll break, however earnest I might be in proposing them to myself, and for new strategies. For instance, I usually resolve to keep myself as fresh as possible throughout the year, not losing intellectual steam as the term progresses. There is nothing worse than feeling dragged down in April or May, feeling as though you cannot possibly read another student paper or exam. As the school year begins, I always vow to devise fresh ways of keeping my writing alive while I'm teaching, and without damaging one or the other. This is incredibly hard work, of course, and difficult to manage. But I'm forever hopeful that during the upcoming year I will manage to juggle every ball in my complex life, and that I won't long for another year, for a fresh chance to do it better the next time around.

But thank God for academic time, with its endless supply of fresh starts. In so many occupations, time simply rolls on and on, with nothing to look forward to but the death of one's immediate superior, the odd bonus or perhaps a brief, untroubling illness. (I still savor the occasional cold, when I'm too sick to go into the college but not so ill that I can't lie in bed, drink tea, and read.) In the academy, time is oddly and infinitely retrievable. The slate is (in theory) wiped clean in September, and one is given a fresh packet of crayons, a blank notebook. The clock is rewound, and the faces before one never seem to age (except in faculty meetings, where only those who never question anything are without deep lines in their foreheads.) While feelings of guilt over past failures may linger, one can redeem them. That's what beginnings are for.

My Life in School

For over 30 years I've made a life of teaching. Now that I'm within sight of the end of this occupation, or preoccupation, I find it alluring to think about what I did or didn't accomplish, what I might have done better, what I might like to do in the years left to me in the classroom. I find myself thinking, too, about my early teachers, wondering what they taught me, and what I found useful—or definitely unhelpful—in their examples. Having become aware of how little decent writing exists on the art of teaching, I've got some hope that my reflections will help those at the beginning of their work in the profession.

It still seems odd to me that I wound up in teaching. As a student in high school and college, I often felt that a teacher was someone who got between me and my reading. I used to believe that teachers unfairly attempted to control the nature and pace of my work, my rate and quality of retention, the ultimate direction of my thoughts. I considered these things private matters, and still do. (If a book was listed on a syllabus, I naturally veered away from it, not toward it.) Fortunately for me, a few teachers seemed different from the rest. They were genuinely and deeply interested in what they taught, and I knew they would be focused on the material before them even if the class suddenly dissolved before their eyes. This material, this subject, was their life. And they never tried to control my thinking; rather, they led me with considerable subtlety in directions I found challenging, if not always congenial. In short, for reasons too difficult to explain, or impossible to explain, I needed a light touch, and they provided it.

I was always suspicious of the classroom as a testing ground for intelligence, a place for sorting the "good" from the "bad" students. The idea of the academic world as a place of competition repelled me. To be frank, it still does, and I never feel happy with students or colleagues who seem excessively interested in grading, in putting up barriers to jump across. I hate exams, and I find quizzes an annoyance—for me as well as the students who must take them. Test-oriented teaching strikes me as anti-educational, a kind of unpleasant game that subverts the real aim of education: to waken a student to his or her potential, and to pursue a subject of considerable importance without restrictions imposed by anything except the inherent demands of the material. The whole direction of education in the United States, with rigid testing of students and, now, even high-school teachers, seems woefully misdirected, and ruinous to learning.

I came by my suspicions about the classroom honestly, I should say. My own family was, in the common parlance, uneducated. That is, they had not submitted to the usual academic rituals for the prescribed length of years. My father, the son of Italian immigrants from Rome and Liguria, quit school at the age of 12 to help the family by working on local farms, picking beans. He later resumed his education to a certain extent, earning the equivalent of a high-school diploma; but he was not, in any real way, "educated." The only book he ever studied seriously was the Bible. My mother dropped out in the ninth grade to work as a waitress in a coffee shop, though she developed a love of reading that never abated. She was highly intelligent, but had no wish to determine the course of my studies. Nor did my father, who let me go my own way. Education was my own business, and I would succeed or fail without much guidance from above—although my parents were certainly committed to the idea that I should be educated, and they supported me consistently.

Alexander Hamilton #19, a working-class elementary school in Scranton, Pennsylvania, perched on a hilltop only a few minutes' walk from my house. My mother had gone there 30 years before me, and it had not been well maintained in the intervening decades. The walls and ceilings were cracked, as were many windows; there was nothing high-tech about any aspect of the school. Its curriculum provided no jump-start on the road to erudition, and there were none of the bells and whistles that one sees at most elementary schools nowadays: gyms and libraries, video machines, computers. Finding the school unpleasant in every way imaginable, I escaped my daily prison house through daydreaming. As might be expected, I struggled through the first six grades, reading and writing without any particular success. A sharply painful shyness overwhelmed me most days, and I rarely answered in class or, for that matter, spent much time talking with anybody. After school, I usually made my way back into the schoolyard, where I shot baskets by myself, occasionally working my way into a pick-up game.

For reasons beyond my understanding, I developed a quiet sense of my own voice and believed I was intelligent—despite what the school system tried to tell me. I vividly recall the transition to West Scranton Junior High, which combined with the senior high to form a complex of several thousand students, most of them obsessed by the football team, which ranked high in the state, in large part because of Cosmo Iacavazzi, a fullback of astounding power and determination.

I used to stand at the edge of the practice field, long after the rest of the team had gone home, to watch Cosmo practice. He fascinated me: a fairly short, highly intelligent and single-minded fellow who seemed never to tire of doing drills. He hammered his body for hours into a padded contraption that absorbed his frontal assault. Fierce, fearless, disciplined in the extreme, able to set high athletic goals for himself, he was quite unlike anyone else around me. I was not, myself, enough of an athlete to aspire to anything like glory; I nevertheless saw that determination was a virtue, and believed that one could achieve interesting results by trying very hard, by keeping one's focus, by refusing to quit.

I was not really able to transfer this lesson in tenacity to the classroom: I simply did not have that kind of tenacity, and still distrusted the academic system. But I often went to the public library after school, having discovered reading almost accidentally in the seventh grade when, during a study hall, I found a copy of *David Copperfield* in the desk where I was sitting and, with nothing better to do, began the first chapter. Something clicked, and I took the book home and finished it. For some years, I read only books recommended to me by Mrs. Godfrey, an elderly librarian with lots of blue hair. I remember reading a lot more of Dickens, as well as Sir Walter Scott, Edgar Allan Poe, John Steinbeck, and Robert Frost—the latter became a passion that has never left me. (In fact, I eventually moved to Vermont because I loved Frost and wanted to live in the physical world he evoked in those poems.) I also read a lot of biographies, eager to see how young men became established in the world. Ben Franklin, Abe Lincoln, and Charles Dickens were my heroes. I liked stories about sports heroes, too, since I played a lot of baseball and basketball. By the time I got into the ninth grade, I felt quite sure that I would become a writer, though I often thought I might do other things as well, with writing as a kind of secret vocation. The profession of teaching never crossed my mind.

A few teachers did manage to snag my wayward attention, and I remember two of them fondly: Jim Loftus and Alberta Mayer. They saw that I was serious and intelligent, though lacking in training, and pushed me in useful directions. It was mostly their attitudes toward the life of the mind that impressed me.

Jim Loftus was a naval veteran of World War II, a fiery Democrat who believed passionately in the teacher's union. He was also an early opponent of the Vietnam War, which in 1965 made him a lone ranger in a place like Scranton, Pennsylvania. I listened anxiously to his antiwar sermons in class, and suddenly understood that teachers were—or might be—people with real feelings, that ideas mattered to them, and that these ideas could cut against the social grain. It took me a little while, but I eventually came to share Jim's feelings about this war. Jim was a quiet teacher, with a cool, bemused stare that I often emulate. He regarded himself as a world-weary intellectual who had somehow to put up with students, and I liked this approach. I liked his sarcasm and skepticism, which he barely disguised. He called me "Mr. Parini" in class, with a slightly ironic twang in his voice. I liked that, too, and I find it useful at times to refer to a student with a title. (There is a girl in my current senior seminar whom I always refer to as The Baroness.)

On the other hand, Miss Maher, my senior English teacher, who brought Eliot and Yeats into my life, was never ironic. She could be sly and superior, but without the distance that was part of the Loftus approach. Her rapid-fire talk and obvious enthusiasm for the literature she taught provided a perfect model for me in my early years in the classroom: I have made a habit of enthusiasm, and always manage to find texts to discuss that warrant this approach. It works, I must say: Students often say how much they appreciate a teacher who has passion for the subject, and one who communicates the reasons for this passion. "Literature," Miss Maher used to say, or declaim, "provides options for living." I believed her, and still do. In fact, I often say the very same thing to students, and I try to make them see that literary texts—poems, novels, and plays—can suggest directions for thought and action that may not have occurred to them yet.

When I think back to my bumpy ride through grade school and, to a lesser extent, my rocky years in junior high, I find it difficult to explain what went so wrong. Physiological and psychological issues played some role in my inattention, my distraction, my inability to read and cipher. Nowadays school psychologists isolate any number of problems, including dyslexia and various attention disorders. I know my attention was hard to attract, and most teachers would have found me a tough nut to crack.

Things began to break my way in about the eighth or ninth grade, when my reading skills leaped forward, and I began to write at home in the evenings and on weekends for pleasure: poems, stories, essays. I don't know why I suddenly began to write; there was no obvious stimulus for this. But the impulse came, and I made use of it. I even found, to my amazement, that I could do higher forms of math, such as geometry, more easily than I could do basic arithmetic. I scraped through subjects that failed to hold my interest, such as most basic sciences, and focused on things that did: English and American literature, history and politics, French. I spent a lot of time with the Thespian Club, acting in plays. (I discovered that I had a genuine ability to hold the attention of large numbers of people, and here, I suspect, lay the foundations of my teaching self.) Despite an uneven record—my transcript read like a bad cardiograph—I squeaked into Lafayette College, my first choice, and felt quite dazzled by my good luck. I was the first member of my family to step onto a college campus, and there were some kudos there.

Lafayette captured my imagination from the outset. It was a beautiful, small college founded in 1826, and the campus was clustered on a hilltop overlooking Easton and the Delaware River. For the first time, I was around people who liked to talk seriously about literature and politics, and I sat around in my freshman dorm at night until two in the morning, discussing Big Ideas. I began to think of myself as somebody with intellectual aspirations, and was quite overwhelmed when Paul Goodman came to the campus. He gave a talk to a small group on something like "the life of the mind," and I was impressed. I bought and read half a dozen of his books, including *Growing Up Absurd* and *The Community of Scholars.* Goodman suggested that I read Joseph Campbell, and I got my hands on *The Hero with a Thousand Faces*, which I read avidly.

My freshman year proved tough going, however. I had never really concentrated on the details of writing in a way that any self-respecting college English teacher would find acceptable. I spelled like Scott Fitzgerald and punctuated like William Faulkner, which is to say that chaos reigned in these areas. I had never learned to study systematically, and the whole of knowledge seemed to me confusing, even beyond my grasp. The truth is, I could barely stay awake in the face of a subject that didn't hold my interest, and easily zoned out. Fortunately, I was curious about the world and found that some of what I was asked to read actually had a bearing on things that mattered to me. I made my way through books on American history and politics with particular attention, trying to figure out how the United States had got itself into its current, unhappy situation—as in the Vietnam War, which became a preoccupation after about 1966 and colored everything I read.

My reading tastes expanded to include political theory and international relations, though I never took courses in these subjects. I joined various organizations against the war, such as

Students for a Democratic Society. I attended study groups and political rallies, and began to read *The Nation* and other periodicals. My main intellectual life still occurred mostly outside of the boundaries of the classroom, although I did find some of my courses engaging and was learning to adhere to the conventions of spelling, punctuation, and syntax. I was also learning to make an argument on paper: mostly because I had arguments about the war that I felt I must try to make.

One of the crucial decisions I made at this time was to spend my junior year abroad, at St. Andrews in Scotland. I knew precious little about either Scotland or this particular university when I set sail, on a small ocean liner from Genoa, in the autumn of 1968. I remember that I was reading Isaiah Berlin's study of Karl Marx, a book on the history of Czechoslovakia, and *The Stranger* by Albert Camus on the transatlantic crossing, which took six or seven days. At about this time, I began to keep a journal, a cheap spiral notebook in which I wrote the rough drafts of poems, odd prose paragraphs, titles for books I might one day write, quotations, and miscellaneous jottings. In the decades since, I've never not had a journal in hand, and I usually write something every day in its pages. Then and now, I often copy out favorite poems by other writers, or bits of poems. I often write snatches of overheard conversations, too—a consequence, perhaps, of writing in restaurants.

I recall with pristine clarity that evening when I arrived in St. Andrews on the train from Leuchars Junction (a railway link no longer in existence). I paced up and down the three main streets of the town, all of which converge at the ruined cathedral, and St. Rules Tower: a haunting outcrop of medieval architecture. I went down to the harbor below the cathedral, and walked out to the end of a stone pier, and sat looking across an expanse of black water, a sky filled with stars. The air was salty and cool, and I could hear the water crashing in the rocks. It was all so bracing and, curiously, familiar, even though I had never been to such a place before. St. Andrews felt like home right from the beginning.

My taste for poetry and fiction deepened considerably during my junior year. There was an active intellectual culture in my residence hall, St. Regs, and I listened eagerly to fellow students as they talked about Eliot and Yeats. I remember in particular a night when an older student came into my room and read, with a sonorous Scottish accent, "The Love Song of J. Alfred Prufrock." His reading of that poem, in a suitably dramatic voice, made more of an impression on me than any course I had ever taken in poetry, and to this day I regard reading aloud to my students from poetry and fiction as one of the essential things I do in the classroom. What I try to convey in these readings is *tone*, the attitude of the speaker in the text toward the material at hand. Over the years, a surprising number of students have told me that they learned to read closely by listening to me read aloud.

During my first term in St. Andrews, I was fortunate to have a young tutor called Tony Ashe, whose seminars were occasions for alert, forceful confrontations with a wide range of texts, from Pope and Wordsworth to Eliot and Yeats. Tony introduced me to Gerard Manley Hopkins, a poet who seemed almost to reinvent the physical world with his language, in his journals as well as his poems, giving it freshness and tangibility. Tony treated each member of his seminar with a respectful diffidence, expecting students to say intelligent and serious things, and to discover ways that the text at hand embodied, or bodied forth, experience. He was working in the New Critical mode, having studied at St. Andrews and Oxford during the fifties and early sixties, when Empson and Leavis were still in high fashion. In keeping with this tradition, he often stripped the poems of their historical/biographical contexts, much as I. A. Richards had done at Cambridge in the twenties. In retrospect, I see that my teaching life began there, around a highly polished oak table in Castle House, where the tall windows looked out over the icy North Sea and a huge, cobalt sky. I found myself being articulate in a classroom for the first time, discussing matters that felt dear and relevant to my intellectual and spiritual life. The intensity of this experience was transforming.

I developed a taste for literary criticism that year, reading Cleanth Brooks and Robert Penn Warren, John Crowe Ransom, Allen Tate, Leavis and Empson, and many others. I also read my way through many volumes by Bertrand Russell, whose opposition to the Vietnam War had caught my attention. His three-volume *Autobiography*, which I found riveting, became a touchstone of my intellectual and emotional life. The first volume opens with a sentence I have learned by heart: "Three passions, simple but overwhelmingly strong, have governed my life: the longing for love, the search for knowledge, and unbearable pity for the suffering of mankind." I cannot, to this day, imagine more noble, or useful, passions. At this time I also read many of Russell's provocative essays on a wide range of topics, and began to model my prose on his, forging a style that favored clarity and balance, a certain lightness and briskness, concision as well as concreteness. Instinctively, I disliked the meandering, obscure, ungainly prose of Leavis, much as I have disliked much of the criticism written in the United States over the past two decades. I still reread Russell once in a while, just to ground myself again in his firmness of intellect and moral courage. (Of course I've read the recent biographies of Russell, and know he was hardly a model specimen of integrity, but I stick by that sentence of his. His ideals were high; in failing to meet them, he was only human.)

I returned to Lafayette with a sense of myself as an intellectual, a person for whom ideas and texts were central. I also began to think of myself as a poet, having taken to verse-writing with a feeling of vocation while abroad. Though I had written poems in high school and during my first two years at college, I didn't take myself as someone for whom the writing of poetry was a necessary activity. Now I did. So I chose courses in my senior year with a view to deepening my education as a poet. At the center of this was a year-long course on the history of Western literature with a luminously intelligent professor called W. Edward Brown, then in his late sixties. He had been a classicist by training, with a graduate degree from Yale. He read French, Italian, German, Spanish, and Russian literature in the original with apparent ease, and wrote a brilliant history of Russian literature before the nineteenth century. He had also translated Rilke into verse, and written a good deal about Italian poetry. He was, I think, the most scholarly man I have ever met.

The first major text I studied with Brown was by Homer, for whom he had a particular affinity. He read aloud in Greek, translating as he went. I recall reading *The Iliad* through the night, in the Lattimore translation, with tears in my eyes, stunned by the beauty and tragic vision embodied in those pages. We moved on through *The Odyssey*, through Virgil and Dante, Cervantes and Goethe. "I'm giving you an aerial view of Western literature," Dr. Brown would tell the class. "When you graduate, you can begin to visit these places on the ground. The view will shift, but at least you will know where the mountain peaks are, and where you can find the capitals of each province." This was old-fashioned stuff, but intensely stimulating.

I would sometimes go to Dr. Brown's house in the afternoons, for tea. He lived alone, in a massive house full of books. This was my first glimpse of the scholar's life, and I was dazzled. I told him about the critics I had brought back from Scotland with me: Empson, Leavis, and Richards. He shook his head disdainfully and put Eric Auerbach and Ernst Curtius into my hands. "This is the best of modern criticism," he said. He explained to me about what he called "philological or historical criticism," and he urged me to think in broad terms, to historicize works of literature, to study a genre in its development from era to era. He also introduced me to George Saintsbury, the great Scottish historian of literature, who had written a three-volume history of English prosody.

Oddly enough, Dr. Brown was not a gifted performer in the classroom. He read from densely prepared lectures, rarely pausing to make a point stick, or changing the pitch of his voice. He would cough—or clear his throat with a husky rumble—every two minutes or so. This was wildly irritating. But his erudition and passion for literature and ideas were obvious, and students admired him, even worshipped him. The main lesson I learned from this important teacher was that content matters more than anything else. You cannot fake the substance of a course, and must always teach from the center of your material, trusting the material to carry the class forward, to stimulate the students. I have had periods in my teaching life when I didn't trust the material, and—believe me—students noticed. There was something evasive about my teaching, especially in the early years. I have always used the memory of Edward Brown as a way of reminding myself to stick with the core intellectual content of each class, and let the truth and beauty of the material carry its own weight. In some ways, the best teachers are those who step aside, letting the subject dominate, letting it shimmer. This takes skill and faith, but it remains the only way to succeed as a teacher.

I took courses on Shakespeare and Milton with another inspired teacher, James Lusardi. A tall, theatrical man who favored turtleneck sweaters and suede shoes, he would read long passages from the plays, acting out the various parts, changing his voice to match the character with apparent ease; he recited *Paradise Lost* with a peculiar verve, and I cannot read that epic to this day without hearing the lines in Jim's resonant voice. We met for seminars at his house just off campus, drinking bottles of beer as we discussed *Lear* or *Samson Agonistes* well past the allotted time. Often, I would stay after the rest of the class had gone, sitting at his kitchen table over a bottle of gin. I anxiously showed him my latest poems. He always began our private sessions by reading my poetry aloud, just as he had read Shakespeare or Milton. That he took my poetry seriously was, of course, a boost. I began to take myself as seriously, learning that one must always treat a student's work with the utmost seriousness. (I often make a point of reading a student's poems aloud in my office: the experience, for them, can be unusually helpful.)

The war in Vietnam escalated, horribly and wastefully. I marched on Washington and helped to organize protests at Lafayette and around northeastern Pennsylvania. I spoke at rallies and debated pro-war students in public forums. It inspired me that my professors felt as outraged about the injustice and cruelties of this war as I did. They frequently brought up the war in literature classes, regarding the great writers—Homer, Virgil, Milton, Wordsworth—as human touchstones, and therefore relevant to the conduct of life in the twentieth century. I remember reading aloud from Wordsworth's *Prelude* to a small circle of friends, then discussing his attitudes to the French Revolution and comparing them to our feelings about Vietnam. I loved, in particular, the seventh book, which in part concerns the young poet's visit to revolutionary France, about which he wrote: "Bliss was it in that dawn to be alive / But to be young was very Heaven!"

My grades in my senior year spiked upward with my newly discovered commitment to intellectual things. It seemed natural that I should continue my studies, and that I should return to St. Andrews, where I hoped to reconnect with Tony Ashe. The graduate program there suited me: one simply wrote a thesis, working mostly on one's own.

I returned to St. Andrews in late September, eager to start on my graduate work—the B.Phil. thesis on Gerard Manley Hopkins. The chairman of the English Department—my supervisor—was called, simply and deferentially, The Professor. In those days, there was only one professor, the person who ran the department. This was true of every department: one professor per subject. Everyone else worked as his assistant. In the English Department, this included Tony Ashe. We all talked with a kind of bemused affection about The Professor, A. F. Falconer. He was a tiny, wizened man with long hair and a distracted manner. He looked a lot like Shakespeare in the famous etching: a thin face, a long nose, a high forehead. His baggy, pinstriped suits seemed to have been made for a man much taller and fatter, the sleeves coming down over his palms, the cuffs billowing over his shoes. He was a Shakespearean scholar of no great repute, the author of an eccentric book called *Shakespeare and the Sea*, in which he argued that during the lost years of the Bard's life he must have been an officer in the Royal Navy, otherwise he could not have known so much about the habits of seagoing types, such as Othello. A wonderfully ambiguous blurb on the dust jacket suggests that this book should be "put on every seagoing man's bookshelf, and kept there." The Professor had followed up this tome with an even more bizarrely idiosyncratic study: *A Glossary of Gunnery and Naval Terms in Shakespeare*.

In truth, I liked old Falconer, and would frequently stop by for chats in his windy office in Castle House. His darkly negative views on such authors as Joyce and Virginia Woolf were, I admit, amusing. When I suggested that students might enjoy *Dubliners*, he responded gravely: "I quite agree, but it might encourage them to read more Joyce." He considered C. S. Lewis "a great fraud who had jumped on the Christian bandwagon" and adored the novels of Hugh Walpole, "surely the best of the moderns." He claimed that, among the modern poets, Robert Bridges led the pack. "His *Testament of Beauty* surpasses *The Waste Land*," he frequently said. He was, I see in retrospect, in the early stages of Alzheimer's when I worked with him, which may account for the oddity of his comments on my work. I remember giving him a chapter of my thesis in which the word "masturbation" appeared. Falconer drew a thick line through the offensive word and wrote above it, in his meticulous hand, "self-directed pleasure." His favorite poet, apart from the Bard of Avon, was Rupert Brooke, that Adonis among poets who lost their lives in the Great War.

Although officially a student of Falconer's, I was in reality working with Tony Ashe, who guided me briskly and intelligently through my B.Phil. thesis on Hopkins and my Ph.D. thesis on Theodore Roethke. When I complained to him about the unpleasant conditions in the postgraduate dorm where I was living, he invited me to occupy the top floor of his house: a suite of rooms with a separate bath. Eagerly, I moved in with him and his wife, Sue, and their four young children. I became a member of their family.

Lunchtime at the Ashe house on North Street was always a rambling seminar, and various members of staff and friends— mostly graduate students like myself—brought bits and pieces to the meal: cans of tuna, loaves of bread, hunks of cheddar, packets of instant soup. For dessert, we had what we called "chemical pudding"—a sweet, glutinous substance that came in various pastel shades. We talked, and joked, about everything—from literature and current events to history and the arts; I picked up an immense amount of historical and literary knowledge at those lunches. When literary visitors came through town to lecture or read, they would often join us for lunch, swelling the crowd, adding a dimension to the conversation. Among the poets who stomped through the blue front door at North Street were Alastair Reid, Seamus Heaney, Edwin Morgan, Stephen Spender, Iain Crichton Smith, Norman MacCaig, Philip Hobsbaum, and Anne Stevenson.

It was during my first term as a graduate student, in 1970, that Professor Falconer called me unexpectedly one night to ask if I would be willing to teach a group of second-year students, who were mainly focused on English poetry in the eighteenth century. I readily agreed, happy with the prospect of leading a discussion on James Thomson or Alexander Pope. Beginning in the Martinmas term, I met twice a week with a small class and served as their tutor, meeting once a week individually with each student to discuss a handwritten, three-page essay on the text of the week. During the second term, Candlemas, the scope of my teaching widened when I was invited to give a number of public lectures to the entire second-year class, which must have numbered 200 or so students. My first lecture, in a freezing hall dating from the fifteenth century, was on Hopkins, and it was delivered word-for-word from a carefully typed manuscript; even the quotations were typed out. I continued to lecture and run student discussions and tutorials throughout the year, without pay or official status. During my second year in graduate school, The Professor managed to get me a teaching fellowship, which carried a modest stipend. I was off and running.

In the course of five years, I conducted countless tutorials, led seminars, and gave formal lectures on Chaucer and Shakespeare, Ben Jonson's plays, the Metaphysical poets, Pope and Sterne, Austen, Wordsworth, Hardy, Eliot, and Yeats—just to name a few of the major figures I was asked to teach. I remember once having to present a series of lectures to the Junior Honors Class on medieval Scots poetry because the usual specialist on this subject was ill. (My Scots accent provided endless amusement for the students, but I insisted on reading large passages of the verse aloud.) I somehow managed all of this, sometimes badly, and got my graduate education by reading books in order to teach them. I was encouraged by colleagues, a feisty group of young dons, to read widely among the popular critics of the day. I also read the critical work of the major poet-critics: Ben Jonson, Dr. Johnson, Coleridge, Matthew Arnold, and Eliot. Eliot, in particular, filled me with an almost visceral excitement as I annotated the margins of his fierce, prim, erudite essays. (I reread *The Sacred Wood* every year or so, just to reconnect with that energy.) Perhaps in emulation of Eliot (and Pound, whom I also read closely), I attended lectures and seminars in the Classics Department, studying Latin and Greek literature with some first-rate scholars.

Always, my teaching and reading went hand-in-glove with my self-education as a poet. I read and discussed poems to better understand how poets achieved certain rhetorical effects, and to see what sorts of poems could be made from certain subjects. I loved scanning poems, getting down to the nitty-gritty of versification. The mechanics of verse composition, and the use of various formal patterns, became second nature to me. I was able to use this recently acquired expertise in writing on Hopkins and Roethke, both of whom were attentive to the conventions of poetry. I liked the notion of the poet as Maker, and took seriously the craftsmanship involved. I must have written hundreds of mediocre sonnets and villanelles, sestinas, and such, always confident that no work in this vein is pointless; the mediocre poem makes possible, in time, the good poem.

I usually wrote poems in the morning, going to a tea shop around the corner, working in a cheap spiral notebook. When I wasn't writing or teaching or socializing, I worked on my research thesis, pausing to read for weeks at a time in directions that seemed relevant to my work. For instance, I read a good deal of Jung and Freud in the early seventies, since Roethke was reading them and using their ideas in his poetry. I acquired the habit of bringing up subjects in my classes that connected in direct ways to my reading and thinking, aware I could never keep my mind focused on the class at hand if I weren't genuinely working through my ideas *with* the class. When I lectured, I allowed my preoccupations to dominate the material, preferring to talk about what really interested me over what was prescribed. Though I cannot be sure, I think that students responded well to those classes. At least those who have remained in touch have said as much.

I came to admire the British attitude toward teaching. University students were assumed to have reached adulthood, and left to their own devices. What the teacher provided was a model of intellectual curiosity. Lectures were extremely well prepared but certainly optional for students. Seminar discussions were invariably focused on a particular text. Tutorials centered on whatever writing a student had done. I don't doubt that there was a lot of bad teaching happening in the university—isn't there always?—but I had a nose for bad teachers and avoided them; I would jettison a course of lectures quickly if I discovered the teacher was boring or ill prepared. I myself gave lectures that were meticulously worked out, reading my first lectures verbatim, pausing here and there to provide a further example. I enjoyed the aspect of performance, of what Wittgenstein called "ostentation," or "showing," and would attempt to "act out" a poem or scene from a play or novel. It also seemed important to entertain the student audience, so I frequently planted prompts for jokes in the margins of lectures or texts. Quite recently, I found an old copy of Wordsworth's *Selected Poems* with an ominous note beside "The Old Cumberland Beggar": TELL THE ONE ABOUT THE FIRE IN THE NURSING HOME. Moments of comic relief, offering a definite break from the flow of the instruction, seemed crucial in holding the attention of a big class. To this day, I ad-lib jokes or amusing anecdotes at various points along the way, just to make sure I have the attention of the students, who have come to expect hard laughs as well as serious intellectual work in any course of mine.

I sometimes ventured beyond St. Andrews for academic experiences. Once, I spent several months in Oxford, doing research on Hopkins, and managed to attend some good lectures there. I had met Sir Isaiah Berlin, the great intellectual historian, when he lectured in St. Andrews, and made further contact with him in Oxford. He was a brilliant talker and charismatic lecturer: I heard him lecture many times, and often sat in his rooms in All Souls. Our conversations ranged widely over the fields of literature, politics, and philosophy, and he often sent me racing to the bookstore. I attended seminars by the philosopher P. F. Strawson, whose fiercely no-nonsense approach to the subject at hand could be daunting. I had many fine conversations about biographical research and teaching with Richard Ellmann, the biographer of Joyce, Yeats, and Wilde. Oxford made a strong impression on me, and I returned there as a visiting fellow at Christ Church with considerable excitement in 1993–1994, renewing my friendship with Berlin and others.

One of the interesting friendships I developed in Scotland was with Philip Hobsbaum, a poet and critic of considerable scope and ability, who held a poetry workshop on Sunday nights at his large flat. I would come, tremulously, with a poem for discussion. I think I learned a good deal about how to run a workshop from Philip, who had himself studied with Leavis and Empson. He assumed that the text before the group deserved the most precise and rigorous criticism, and examined the language and structure of the text with an intensity that left the person being "workshopped" breathless with anxiety and awe but grateful, in most cases. His methodical approach to reading a poem, paying attention to every comma or colon, made one alert to punctuation as road signs for the reader. He might select a word—usually an adjective or adverb—and question its appropriateness. He would read a line over and over, aloud, so that the group could hear the rhythm in various ways, often showing how slight changes in syntax could radically improve the meaning of a line, enhancing its tonal exactness. Despite the ferocious quality of his critiques, Philip seemed perfectly neutral, wanting neither to praise nor blame the person under scrutiny. It was assumed that the task at hand was a professional one, and that we were all in the muck together, trying to learn to use words, to say things well, to make serious (or comic) points with as much force as we could muster.

Closer to home, in St. Andrews, I had a mentor and good friend in Alastair Reid, the Scottish poet and translator. I often cycled out to his cottage by the North Sea, bearing a rough draft of a poem in my rucksack. We would sit side by side in his kitchen at Pilmour Cottage, his stone house overlooking the Old Course, as he dissected my latest effort. He would "correct" my poem, as he said. I sat quietly and watched the language transform before my eyes, the weak adverbs absorbed into stronger verbs, the superfluous or boring adjective erased, contained in a stronger noun. Alastair taught by showing: ostentation, once again. He might cross out a weak phrase and invent a better one. He might rearrange or cancel lines or whole stanzas, refusing to treat any language as sacred. He questioned diction, tone, turns of phrase. His ear was flawless, and I learned how to write in the musical phrase, how to listen to my own poem.

Alastair worked his way through various poems and poets with me. I still recall quite vividly an afternoon when I complained that I did not really understand Yeats's poem "Among School Children." He took me through the poem, stanza by stanza, giving me various possibilities for interpretation. It was stunning but modest as well, paying close attention to the words themselves. He showed me how the seemingly unrelated stanzas fit together, reinforced and reinterpreted the stanzas that went before. He read aloud that sonorous final stanza, and talked about the summary images: the tree, which cannot be separated into its various parts: leaf, blossom, bole. Or the dancer that becomes the dance, the creator so merged with the activity of making meaning that one cannot separate them. Poem and poet. Dance and dancer. The poem became an intimate part of my own psychology, and I look forward to teaching the poem at least once a year. When I do, I hear Alastair talking:

O chestnut tree, great-rooted blossomer,
Are you the leaf, the blossom or the bole.
O body swayed to music, O brightening glance,
How can we know the dancer from the dance?

I returned to the United States uncertainly, taking my first "real" job at Dartmouth in Hanover, New Hampshire. I had landed this job during an interview at the MLA convention in New York the previous winter—an interview that had obviously gone well.

An interview is, of course, a command performance, and there is only one show. You have to present yourself convincingly. This means having a sense of your audience, which isn't always easy. It means reading the expressions on the faces of your interviewers and interpreting their body language. It means convincing them that you would make an appealing and supportive colleague, a good teacher, and a productive scholar: in that order. I've been on many hiring committees over the years, and I'm quite sure that the first thing one asks oneself is, Can I live with this person for the next 20 years? One looks, as might be expected, for academic competence. But one also looks for good humor, a sense of grace and generosity, an ease of being. I am always turned off, as an interviewer, by a sense of dishonesty as well. An impression of authenticity is essential. But authenticity has many sides, and I prefer—as do most interviewers—a candidate who conveys a genuine impression of being a good person, an amiable and interesting colleague, with agility of mind. The nature of the candidate's academic work is, frankly, secondary—although I would never support hiring a person who does not show real passion for his or her work as a scholar or writer.

Once at Dartmouth, I spent more time with students than colleagues, especially at first. Being only a few years older than most of those who sat in my classes, I felt very much on their level, and my social life occurred largely among them. As a result, I had an extremely difficult time trying to find my teaching persona, an authoritative voice in the classroom. It felt as though little of my experience thus far in life had prepared me for Dartmouth, where knowledge seemed heavily packaged in discrete courses that were out of touch with each other. The students seemed terribly goal oriented, and that goal was Wall Street or General Motors. I still thought of teaching as "the common pursuit of true judgment," a phrase of Eliot's, but I couldn't quite match the ideal with the reality.

During my first year of teaching, I was handed two sections of freshman English, which at Dartmouth was called English 5. It was assumed that students coming to an Ivy League school could write decently; for the most part they could. So there was little in the course that would remind anyone of those basic composition sections at state universities. The main text in English 5 was Milton's *Paradise Lost*—a fine idea, in fact, because that epic poem pulls into its vast orbit the whole range of mythology and literature from classical times through the early modern period. It presents a number of moral issues, raises issues of power in male/female relationships, and puts a lot of controversial theological and philosophical issues on the line, such as questions about determination—

a subject that makes for lively classroom discussions. Students feel wildly intimidated at the outset, unable to hear the language, with its archaisms and complex rhetoric. With just a little help from the prof, they quickly learn how to read this daunting text, and they almost always come away with a pleasurable feeling, having confronted a difficult masterwork and mastered it. It sets them up nicely for a successful time in college, where they will face complex material again and again.

I had read Milton's epic closely as an undergraduate, and welcomed the chance to discuss it with students. The Dartmouth kids were, as one might expect, bright and eager to please, although few of them were oriented toward ideas or scholarship; there was little self-scrutiny, which surprised me, having been a student during the late sixties, when my peers were heavily involved in self-examination. I found almost no political awareness among my students, which also dismayed me. So much had changed in such a brief time. For my purposes, however, the students in English 5 wrote fairly well, and there was lots of lively discussion in the classroom. Being immature, I identified with them on many levels, developing a very casual persona, more like that of an older brother who wished them well in their efforts to understand literature than a lordly teacher, somebody they should revere or emulate. I'm sure that sometimes I seemed downright silly, and often left the classroom feeling oddly out of place, hung up between two worlds.

In addition to English 5, I was handed a large lecture course on modern British and American poetry—my favorite subject. Here I was able to draw on my graduate research on Hopkins as well as my abiding interest in Eliot, Yeats, Frost, and Stevens. I cringe, however, when I think back on my performances. I worked from extremely elaborate teaching notes, often reading word-for-word, as I had done in Scotland. Students occasionally seemed bored by my lectures, and I felt anxious when I saw them gazing out the window or nodding off. I wore a dozen or more different personae in front of classes, and these rarely fit very well. I often experienced an eerie sense of disconnection from the class, and felt inadequate as a teacher.

There was, at the time, an extroverted style of lecturing at Dartmouth that seemed especially popular in the English Department. I had one colleague for whom each lecture was a major performance: he would stand before a mirror at home and recite his lecture from memory, the whole damn thing, watching himself perform. He had elaborate rhetorical gestures, and sometimes broke into tears when reciting a passage from a particularly moving text. Another colleague worked in the mode of Wittgenstein, thinking aloud before the class, gulping huge silences, pacing around the room like a caged lion. He might raise his voice to a shout or drop to a whisper within the boundaries of a single sentence. When inspiration struck, the whole earth seemed to shake in Hanover, New Hampshire. He was widely regarded, by students and faculty alike, as a genius. I attended a few of these lectures and agreed with them that he had a marvelous sense of audience and remarkable ways of bringing ideas, and texts, to life. His intellectual gifts were, I could see, formidable.

Nevertheless, I preferred a cooler, more British approach, and considered myself a "common-sense" teacher, someone who casually but effectively presented the material at hand. In my heart of hearts, I feared that I was neither intelligent enough nor as well prepared as colleagues who had been through graduate programs at Yale and Princeton. My education had been ad hoc, personal, and far less systematic than theirs. I was also up against my larger ambition: I wanted to write poems and criticism, perhaps even fiction. Yet teaching had proven wildly time consuming: I spent late nights rereading the texts I had to teach the next morning. Often I poured over student papers, afraid that I would miss something obvious, unsure how to grade this work, which often appeared neat and formally sufficient but utterly banal, uninspired. I often slept badly, worried about my performance in the classroom. I felt even worse after English Department meetings, where I rarely opened my mouth, and when I did so, I said stupid things. With good reason, I wondered if I could ever manage to write anything in this context.

In the course of my first year, I developed a routine (not unlike what had served me well in Scotland) that continues to guide me through the day. I would go to a local diner for breakfast, taking with me a volume of poems by a favorite poet. I also carried a spiral notebook and a pen. Over coffee and bagels, I would read and write drafts of poems, rework poems, or just take notes on the poetry I was reading. Soon I filled notebook after notebook with verses, some of which (often late at night, before going to bed) I would type out and send to magazines. I remember one miraculous time in the late seventies when my poems were accepted by *Poetry*, *The Atlantic*, and *The New Yorker* in the course of three days. These acceptances spurred me on, and I spent hours and hours reworking poems, retyping them, sending them around to friends for criticism, trying to get them published.

I shared my hopes for myself as a writer and methods of composition with my students, and my frankness held their interest, especially those who wanted to become writers themselves. Several students worked closely with me, outside of class, and it seemed as though we were all in this together, trying to become writers. I was just the lucky one with the job and a few incidental publications to my credit. My apartment was a place where young writers came to chat, drink wine, and talk for hours about poetry and fiction. It often struck me that most of my "teaching" took place outside of the actual classroom. Indeed, I very much preferred this kind of informal teaching. I still do.

Publish or perish was a dictum I took seriously, so I decided to revise my doctoral thesis on Theodore Roethke and the tradition of

American Romanticism. I remember scrolling a blank page into the typewriter in my tiny study in Hanover, writing the title on the top of the page, and then beginning to rewrite my thesis from scratch. Whenever I wasn't teaching or sitting in my office with students, I seemed to be writing. This continued for a couple of years, and the writing seemed to go well, but I often felt unhappy and wondered if I could or should continue with a career inside the academy. I had not become comfortable as a gatekeeper for corporate America. Teaching often felt like a duty, more obligation than inspiration. What I wanted was the freedom to write whatever I wished to write, whenever I wished to write it. I began to resent time spent getting ready for class, and did whatever I could to make preparations less time consuming. Not surprisingly, this often backfired, making my classes less productive and, for me as well as my students, less interesting. I wondered if it was really possible to write and teach at the same time.

There is a fine balance that an academic must somehow achieve, balancing writing (or research) on the one hand, and teaching on the other. Ideally, the two should work together. In my life, the balance was off, and I resented my classroom work, even though I usually managed to do a workmanlike job in the classroom. The stress was horrendous, however, given the pressures of the tenure system, which I loathed.

I regarded the older, tenured members of the English Department as judges, not colleagues, and felt watched by them. I'm sure they were not really watching me, but the system was set up in such a way that one could easily become paranoid. Nevertheless, I found there was something I could learn from almost every one of them, and it was interesting to hear them talk, to read their work (if they had published anything), and to try out ideas on them. Over the course of seven years, a few of them became valued friends, but this would have been easier, less pressured, had I not had to worry constantly about the tenure business. My younger colleagues felt pitted against each other, and this was extremely uncomfortable for me. I had no wish to compete with anyone. I was very competitive, of course, but with myself.

The pressure to publish—as much as I could, as quickly as I could—was palpable, or at least that is how I interpreted what my senior colleagues said to me and how my junior colleagues behaved. I worked furiously at my Roethke book, at various articles and reviews for journals. I kept at my poetry as best I could. But the center could not hold, and I often found myself walking to class without a sense of purpose, with fear in my belly. There were, of course, many days when I felt in tune with the class, believing that I was being a helpful, effective teacher. I might well have been. But classes rarely seemed to cohere in ways that satisfied me, and I sometimes felt as though I was wasting my own time and that of my students. I wondered if I should have taken up some other line of work.

One of the places within the curriculum where I felt most comfortable was in creative writing seminars, which at Dartmouth were limited to ten students. We usually met at my apartment, sitting in a circle on the living room floor; we talked over bottles of cheap wine and bowls of potato chips. In this intimate setting, students often became friends. These seminars gave me a lift, as practical criticism was my best hand as a teacher. I modeled these seminars on Philip Hobsbaum's writing group at Glasgow, keeping the text of each student intensely in view, looking for ways to revise that would tighten or clarify the poem or story. Emphasizing concreteness, clarity, and coherence, I could hear Philip's voice in my head as I taught, as well as the voices of Tony Ashe, Jim Lusardi, and others. I often reread essays by Eliot, Leavis, Empson, Yvor Winters, William Wimsatt, and others. Their voices, too, played in my head.

The fantasy of liberating myself once and for all from academic life nevertheless refused to die. The pressure of trying to win tenure kept me on edge, ill-at-ease. I thought I would write better stuff if I could move outside of the academy walls, and thought about those lucky writers who had managed to live without teaching: Hemingway and Fitzgerald, Yeats, Eliot, Stevens. Could a "real" writer exist within these ivy-covered walls? With some whimsy, I decided to write a bestseller, giving me the financial freedom I would need if I did finally decide to quit teaching. Rather compulsively, I rose very early each day and, for an hour or so, worked on my novel, which I called *The Love Run*. It was a story about a beautiful Dartmouth undergraduate who is pursued by a local New Hampshire lad, a "townie." It was fast paced, sexy, and brainless. Unfortunately, it was snapped up by a publisher, who paid well for the privilege of putting my lurid narrative into print.

The administration took badly to my first effort at writing fiction, as did a few senior members of the faculty. Although I was passed for tenure by the English Department, I didn't get past the final stage of the review. The current president of Dartmouth had not been amused by my portrayal of campus life, and the alumni had not found my first efforts at fiction an endorsement for their school. I could (and have) blamed others for my failure to get tenure at Dartmouth, but I realize in retrospect that much of the blame was mine. Although I think I performed adequately in the classroom, even well, I had lost touch with my teaching self; as a consequence, I became less than responsive to student needs and less focused on the material. Quite simply, I had not been able to balance teaching and writing. The whole enterprise of being an assistant professor of English had seemed, after several years, rather beside the point. I lived in my poems, and felt unwilling to compete for tenure in the usual ways. In short, I engineered my own downfall rather masterfully, if unconsciously.

The tenure system is, as everyone knows, deeply flawed. Having worked without tenure for seven years at Dartmouth, and having had tenure at Middlebury College for some two decades, I've seen the upsides and the downsides of the system. People usually get tenure because they have accepted the local institutional standards, whatever these might be. They have learned, by hit or miss, what it takes to succeed with the students in their school. This is no mean feat, and what will pass for excellent teaching at one institution may not measure up at another. They have also managed to rise to a level of scholarly activity (and quality) that satisfies their tenure committees, making them appear promising in some way. This standard varies wildly from place to place and time to time, so it is crucial for a young instructor to figure out what will suffice and what will not. I've seen many sad cases of younger colleagues making a fatal miscalculation in this area, only to find themselves suddenly without tenure, even though they have wonderful teaching credentials. This scenario is, in fact, a cliché by now, but one that young academics seem bound to repeat many times each year throughout the country.

So there I was, in 1981: married, with a child on the way, without a job. Forced to confront reality, I began to reassess myself as a teacher and writer. What did I really want to do with my life? Should I try to write best-selling fiction, full time? Would it make more sense to start a business? Should I move to Hollywood and write screenplays? I remember sitting in my study, looking at the books on my shelf. I saw my own burgeoning stack of notebooks, and my book on Roethke, which had recently appeared and gotten uniformly good reviews in the usual places. I had recently had a collection of poems—*Anthracite Country*—accepted by Random House. But what did I really want?

After weeks of self-scrutiny, I decided that I did, after all, like academic life. I enjoyed the community of scholars, the sense of commitment to ideas, even if I had serious reservations about the uses to which higher education had been put in the United States. I believed there was surely a place for writers of my temperament within the academy, and I considered my gifts for teaching sufficient, and that with proper attention to the task I could become a successful instructor. I knew this would take a good deal of application, but I decided to push forward. I applied for, and soon got, a teaching job at Middlebury College, which was just over the Green Mountains from Hanover. It seemed a very lucky thing that Middlebury appeared, as if from nowhere, to offer another chance.

There is no point in rehashing my career from this point on in any blow-by-blow fashion. In short, I moved to Middlebury, bought a small house in town with my wife, got tenure within a couple of years (without fuss), and eventually became an effective—even popular—classroom teacher. I also managed to write a number of books in various genres: poetry, fiction, criticism, biography. In addition, I published countless book reviews over a period of two decades, largely because I liked earning small sums of cash, which grew increasingly valuable to me as three children arrived. I even managed to write four screenplays and edit a dozen or so books. People often ask me how I did all of this, and I will try to speak frankly about my approach to writing and teaching at the same time. It wasn't easy, but it was fun.

The point here is that a settled, disciplined life is essential for a teacher and a writer. (I often quote to myself Flaubert's dictum on this, which I would roughly translate as "Live like a bourgeois, think like an artist.") It pays to have a routine that actually invites the muse, but this must be an individual thing. My preference is for writing poetry in the early morning, then moving to prose and teaching. I find that having a firm identity as a writer provides a teaching persona that works rather well in the classroom. A class is a performance, and the teacher must be highly self-conscious of the need to craft each lecture or discussion as one might craft a poem or story. The class must have a beginning, a middle, and an end. It must begin somewhere in place and time and proceed to another point, however arbitrary. Students want to be aware of progression, and they need to feel their own development—a sense of having had certain ideas and then found them undermined, challenged, and refashioned. I'm aware that I'm trying to make each student independent of me, capable of confronting a body of material and absorbing it in an individual way, critiquing it, remaking it. The worst thing that I can imagine is for a student merely to accept what I say, without question. My authority in the classroom is, in a way, a fiction; I present myself with authority, but I do so in ways that allow students to confront my point of view, to risk challenging my authority.

Teaching styles differ considerably, and they should. I personally like a casual approach, cultivating a "laid-back" persona, but I keep the focus intensely on the material before me: a piece of student writing, a major text, a topic of discussion. I circle around this material warily, holding it up for inspection, thinking aloud. "Description is revelation," said Wallace Stevens. That seems true of all classroom work, too. The teacher must describe, describe, describe. That description gives way, quite naturally, to evaluation, even revelation. It was Yvor Winters who once noted that life is a process of perpetual revision in the interests of greater understanding, and I try hard to keep this ideal before the students. I revise my own opinions constantly, before their very eyes, basing these revisions on new information, on fresh perceptions, on discovering contradictions in my own thinking or the thinking of my students.

Students have a knack for detecting a lack of sincerity in a teacher. All young teachers should work toward a sense of personal authority and authenticity, while realizing that these human virtues come only with time and practice. Students love it when a teacher appears self-confident, funny, open-minded, agile. They do not want a professor who gazes eagerly in their direction for confirmation.

They want to see confidence. But this confidence means that you are perfectly willing to make mistakes, say stupid things, allow the students to contradict and subvert your ideas. Real authority can be challenged; it *must* be challenged. It seems to me useful to think of each class as an act of revision, as drafts are altered, made more precise, even truer. In this way, teaching (like writing) becomes the pursuit of truth, of "true judgment." An inexperienced teacher often telegraphs his or her own lack of authority by presenting material too firmly, disallowing criticism, refusing to let some things remain in limbo, ill-defined, inchoate. Well-seasoned teachers put the material forward with considerable assurance, but they invite criticism and model the process of revision.

I always wish I could go back to Dartmouth as a young professor again, in my midtwenties, knowing what I know now. I would be so damned self-assured, witty, open to criticism, eager for resistance, ready to acknowledge mistakes and move in better directions, truer directions. I would respect the gifts of each person, allowing them to feel my respect while, at the same time, I would challenge their assumptions, make them uncomfortable. I would find my older colleagues interesting but not intimidating. I would listen to them carefully; but I would express my own views clearly, firmly, without being defensive. I would know how to balance my writing life, my scholarly work, and my social life *with my teaching*. It would all be splendid. But of course this is fantasy. The process of becoming an effective teacher is all trial and error, often quite painful and exhausting. Nevertheless, it cannot hurt a young person entering the profession to keep some of the issues I have raised in mind.

There are no shortcuts to becoming a good teacher, although it probably helps to have good models and to know how to imitate those models while maintaining a sense of your own integrity and respecting your uniqueness as a teacher. A writing voice is developed slowly but from within: you have to acquire a sense of style that is unique, as idiosyncratic as your fingerprints. Experience allows the writer to enhance an individual voice, to make it work efficiently, with enough flexibility to adjust to differing circumstances and demands (such as genre or audience). This is just as true of beginning teachers, who must find their own unique voice, allow it to grow, be shaped, be reshaped. Style is everything in writing and in teaching, and it is never shallow if it's any good. Style is the way a person takes himself, as Robert Frost once suggested. It's a stance toward the world, a way of being.

As I've grown into my work as a teacher, I have felt much less constrained by the walls of the classroom, aware that my work often moves into the open air. I like to spend time outside of the class with students, getting to know them, their needs, their ways of taking themselves. (My family never bats an eyelash when a student turns up for dinner; it's a common occurrence. Students borrow my car, come fishing with me, pick up my children at school when

I can't do it. I treat them as part of my extended family.) I know by now that students regard me as their teacher, not their best friend, and I can accept this at my age. I want them to see me thinking, considering, reconsidering, doubting, remaking myself in their presence. I want them to benefit from the fact that I have thought a good deal more about literature than they have. I also believe I can teach them something about how to live their lives: openly, with a freedom of mind and spirit, a willingness to question assumptions and reformulate notions.

If anything, I think of myself as presenting to students an alternate vision, another way of living in a dangerous world, where the government itself is often corrupt and foolish, ready to sacrifice human liberties and human lives to maintain a good climate for business. In the post–9/11 world, I see my job as having a distinctly political edge, teaching students how to read the world as well as the texts before them. I have stopped worrying about keeping my teaching "apolitical," a concern that haunted me in earlier times. My teaching has acquired a new sense of meaning as I have found ways to speak bluntly about political issues, about world poverty and hunger, about the abuses of American power, about the infringement on our sacred liberties, on the subservience of the press, which in our capitalist system has become increasingly monosyllabic, one-dimensional, fearful of provocation. A teacher's job in the twenty-first century is distinctly political, in that he or she must speak the truth, must find and talk about conflicting truths, must teach habits of resistance that fall under the category of critical thinking.

I am horribly aware that I have no corner on "the truth," of course. But that is exhilarating, liberating. I'm much more willing now than earlier in my teaching life to learn from my students. I have no illusion about my credentials, my erudition, my experience. There are many good things to be said about these qualifications, but I have no special wisdom, and there is a natural wisdom among the young that refreshes me, that startles me, that often forces me to reconsider long-cherished ideas and assumptions. In fact, I continue to work in this profession long after I thought I'd be done with it because I get something valuable *back* from students. Many of them are tough-minded and smart—a lot smarter than I am. It's always fun when they ask me to rephrase a sentence, to support an opinion with hard evidence, to reconsider assumptions made too easily, perhaps long ago.

The problem of balancing a writing life with a teaching life has, quite naturally, preoccupied me over the years. Oddly enough, I seem to get less done on sabbatical leaves than I do while teaching a full load of courses. This may be true because the rhythm of academic life gives a structure to my day, so that I use whatever little bits of free time I have economically instead of making endless cups of tea that I never quite drink. Aware that time is limited, I find myself able to work in the interstices of the day: taking advantage of a half hour here, another there. I know that exams must be graded, papers assigned, read, evaluated, lectures and discussions prepared; I also know that I'll be miserable if I don't write new poems and make progress on essays and prose works. There is a further benefit: I find myself discovering—in the class-room as well as on the page—fresh ways to describe, to embody in language, the world as I find it.

When I look back at roughly three decades of standing on the teacher's side of the desk, I have only a few regrets. I wish I'd been more serious about teaching from the outset, and understood that a teaching life and a writing life can work happily together. I might have avoided years of avoiding myself. I might also have recognized the teaching self as something true, a keenly developed fiction that is not "false." It's simply one mask of many that I wear in the world's eye, and a useful one.

The profession of teaching is a noble one, of course, with roots in the ancient world, as in the brotherhood of Pythagoras, the academic schools, the Peripatetics and Stoics. Great teachers roamed from village to village, acquiring disciples. One thinks mostly of Socrates, the archetypal teacher, with his astonishing openness, his ability to draw from a young mind something worthwhile, something already in place but as yet unformed, inarticulate, even unwelcome, however valuable. I read about these mythical figures with a shrug these days, aware that I am no master. A whole book could be written on the destructive power of masters, who drew innocent seekers into their psychological orbit, only to destroy rather than enlighten them. This is, perhaps, the myth of Faust or the tale of Abelard and Heloise. I shrink from any conception of teaching that too blatantly depends on power plays.

My notion of the ideal teacher is that of *primus inter pares*, with the teacher as lead student. I wish I had understood from the beginning that I was, at heart, a perpetual student: amazed before the world's variety and unworded beauty and frustratingly contradictory nature. As student and teacher in one skin, I work at unraveling the many strands of this world, putting into words its silent beauty, and attempting to resolve the contradictions. Success, in these terms, is always a kind of failure as well, and demands a fresh start, a willingness to ask the fundamental questions in an innocent way, a need to set the whole dialectic in motion once again.

The Teaching Life

A TEACHING VOICE

"Put off that mask of burning gold
With emerald eyes."
"O no, my dear, you make so bold
To find if hearts be wild and wise,
And yet not cold."

"I would but find what's there to find,
Love or deceit."
"It was the mask engaged your mind,
And after set your heart to beat,
Not what's behind."

"But lest you are my enemy,
I must enquire."
"O no, my dear, let all that be;
What matter, so there is but fire
In you, in me?"

W. B. Yeats, "The Mask"

Nobody just walks into a classroom and begins to teach without some consideration of self-presentation, much as nobody sits down to write a poem, an essay, or a novel without considering the voice behind the words, its tone and texture, and the traditions of writing within a particular genre. Voice is everything in literature, playing in the mind of the writer, the ear of the reader; the search for authenticity in that voice is the writer's work of a lifetime. What I want to suggest here is that teachers, like writers, also need to invent and cultivate a voice, one that serves their personal needs as well as the material at hand, one that feels authentic. It should also take into account the nature of the students who are being addressed, their background in the subject and their disposition as a class, which is not always easy to gauge. It takes a good deal of time, as well as experimentation, to find this voice, in teaching as in writing.

For the most part, the invention of a teaching persona is a fairly conscious act. Teachers who are unconscious of their teaching self might get lucky; that is, they might adopt or adapt something familiar—a manner, a voice—that actually works in the classroom from the beginning. Dumb luck happens. But most of the success-ful teachers I have known have been deeply aware that their self-presentation involves, or has involved at some point, the donning of a mask.

This taking on of a mask, or persona (from the Latin word implying that a voice is something discovered by "sounding through" a mask, as in per/sona), is no simple process. It involves artifice, and the art of teaching is no less complicated than any other art form. It is not something "natural," i.e., "found in nature." A beginning teacher will have to try on countless masks before finding one that fits, that seems appropriate, that works to organize and embody a teaching voice. In most cases, a teacher will have a whole closet full of masks to try on for size.

One must get over the foolish notion that a mask is not "authentic," that there is something shameful about "not being yourself." Authenticity is, ultimately, a construction, something invented—much as a particular suit of clothes will feel authentic, or inauthentic, given the context. The notion of the "true" self is romantic, and utterly false. There is no such thing. I've always liked the poem by Pablo Neruda that begins: "My selves are many." Indeed. A biographer, as Virginia Woolf once observed, is lucky to pin down half a dozen selves in a good biography. In reality, there are thousands of selves in every human being. These mingle and shift, mutate, bond, break into parts, reassembling countless times in a single day. This is the reality of selfhood. A beginning teacher must confront this reality from the outset, dispensing with the idea that there is some deep and true self that has an independent existence, that can be fetched from the heart's drawer, displayed easily, without fear, with confidence in its features.

There is wisdom in the poem quoted in my epigraph, "The Mask" by Yeats, a poet who thought deeply about masks, developing a complex doctrine that included a conception of the mask as anti-self. He regarded selfhood as a dialectic that involved a constant negotiation between self and anti-self. In his elegant if somewhat arcane formulation, this dialect assumes the taking on of various antithetical selves: a delicate process in which selves (personae, masks) are tested, then discarded or subsumed into other selves. These selves exist along a continuum that includes one's own visions of self and those of others. It is not just, as Robert Browning once suggested, that we have "two soul-sides, one to face the world with," and one to present in private to the beloved. This doctrine, at least in Yeats, assumes that one actually faces the beloved with a mask as well, that there is no embodiment of voice without the use of a mask, and that the emerging voice may be highly intimate or public but must in some sense "sound through" the figure of the mask. And these masks are many.

I certainly ran through a number of them in my first decade of teaching, first in St. Andrews, then at Dartmouth, then Middlebury. Sometimes I played the pipe-smoking, genial man-of-letters who just happened to wander into the classroom, almost by accident. I would sit on the edge of the desk, my tweed jacket frayed at the collar, my elbows covered in leather patches. I offered jocular (though learned) remarks instead of organized lecture notes, and replied wittily to student questions. I was the embodiment of reason, good sense, moderation, geniality. Several of the teachers I admired over the years had a manner along these lines, but—as I soon enough discovered—I was not a gentleman of the old school; I didn't even own a pipe. I needed a bit more fire, a bit of madness, to lift my performances into the realm of effective teaching. But I went too far in that direction at times, making absurd jokes, letting my hair grow wild, affecting a wild-eyed look. Wearing this mask, I would raise my voice to a near shout at times; at other times, I would whisper. Sometimes I paced like a caged animal or flung chalk at the blackboard. Each time I acted in these extreme disguises, I came away from the class feeling empty and false, something of a fool. My teaching voice, it so happens, exists somewhere between these two poles; but, as I've discovered, it also includes them.

Young college teachers are commonly tossed into the classroom with little or no preparation for what will be the central professional activity of their lives: instructing young people in their discipline, its ways and means. They will often have spent the previous year or two in the library, completing a dissertation: the worst possible preparation for teaching. As a graduate student, I never heard a word spoken about pedagogy; in fact, courses in education were considered beneath contempt, a soft option, full of bogus theorizing. If you were a real scholar, you simply acted like one, imparting your knowledge to a hapless audience of students once you got hired somewhere. It was assumed, wrongly, that if you had managed to get through graduate school and write a doctoral dissertation, you were qualified to enlighten students in your discipline, to teach them how to read and think, to correct their papers, to formulate the principles of a given subject in some useful and effective ways.

One teacher I greatly admired at St. Andrews was Kenneth Dover, a professor of Greek who had achieved international recognition for his brilliant scholarship, which included a book on Aristophanic comedy and an edition of *Clouds*. He remained a productive, highly original scholar for many decades, well into retirement. One of his last books was *Marginal Comment* (1994), a memoir in which he talks a good deal of sense about teaching, among other things. "Nothing was of such importance for my professional life as the discovery that I could teach and that I loved teaching," he writes. "The Army set quite a good example, because it was obvious to me from my first days as a gunner that a remarkable amount of careful thought had gone into methods of instruction and training. Our Physical Training instructors, for example, were in a completely different class from the obtuse creature under whose unfriendly eye I had failed to acquire any gymnastic skills at school, and I have met a disappointingly large number of university lecturers whose clarity of exposition fell far short of the standard expected in gunnery schools."

When I first began to teach at Dartmouth, in 1975, I had not thought much about "methods of instruction." In St. Andrews, as a teaching fellow, I had blundered through tutorials, seminars, lectures, imitating various teachers I admired, including Dover, whose brisk professionalism and aura of sublime detachment had seemed thrilling to me as a student. My teaching went badly at first, especially when I returned from Scotland to the United States to teach at Dartmouth, where I found it very difficult to find a teaching voice. A young man in my midtwenties, I tried on various masks, which rarely fit well. But I was thoroughly unconscious of what I was doing until I paid a visit one afternoon to an old teacher of mine, W. Edward Brown. We went for a long walk up the dirt road behind his house in Chester, Vermont, and talked about teaching.

Brown, who had been one of my favorite undergraduate teachers at Lafayette College, had recently retired and moved to Vermont, where he had kept a summer home for many years. We saw each other regularly, and our conversations about teaching were remarkably frank. On the walk referred to above, I told him about my discomfort in the classroom; I said that I often felt fraudulent, inauthentic. I worried that I would never really find my balance in the classroom, or consider myself a "good" teacher. Brown listened to me carefully—he was a gifted listener—then began to talk about the notion of a "teaching voice." I had never before considered the idea. He suggested that the use of masks by Greek dramatists was something

I should consider in relation to my teaching, and urged me to think about the class as a kind of theater, with the teacher playing the dual role of actor and dramatist.

The actors in Greek tragedies always wore masks, thus telegraphing to the audience the "artificial" nature of the art. A discrete set of masks was available, but these were able to accommodate a vast range of voices; the voices were filtered through these personae, which were largely conventional. In most cases, there was a given cast of characters, related to (for example) a particular myth. The bare plots were largely given, based on myths or heroic tales; even the titles, as one can see from scanning any anthology of Greek literature, were often given; hence, one finds half a dozen plays in the fifth and fourth centuries with the title *Philoctetes*. In each case, the dramatist (Aeschylus, Sophocles, Euripides, Philocles, Achaeus, Antiphon, or Theodectes) rung changes on a familiar story, finding originality from within, not without, the conventional plotline. The writer was thus liberated to create a dramatic voice, or voices, without the ridiculous constraints imposed by the romantic doctrine of originality, which has been so destructive to writers over the past two centuries.

As we walked deep into the countryside of Vermont, with shadows lengthening on the dirt road, Professor Brown talked to me frankly about his own struggles with voice in the classroom, his own attempts to try on various masks, with greater or lesser degrees of success. I listened politely at first, but kept saying that I only wanted to "be myself." Talk about "authenticity" had, of course, been prevalent in the sixties, when I'd been an undergraduate. We had all made our way eagerly through Sartre and Camus, each of whom stressed the notion of life as a quest for an "authentic" self. Ed Brown would have none of this, maintaining firmly that authenticity was a fiction, and that any attempt to communicate, to perform a self in public, entailed taking on a mask, a covering. Without the mask in place, there was nowhere for "voice" to go; it had to speak through something. It needed the mask as a poem needed lines, a play the stage.

That afternoon, I began to think about teaching in a different way, as a conscious act of self-creation, as self-performance. The effect of this idea on my teaching was almost immediate, and salutary, as I began to gain some control over what I was doing. Only a few weeks later, I invited Brown into my classroom to observe my performance, and he was generous enough to come. He sat in the back of the room, taking notes on my "performances," as he called them. We would go back to my apartment afterward and, over a cup of tea, discuss what I had done, and how I might improve. It was extremely helpful. Most of us are left to blunder our way toward a teaching voice that serves us, and our students, well. Unconsciously, we adopt different masks, noticing (or failing to notice) their usefulness. I had little awareness of technique during my first years in the classroom, and the results were predictably variable. It was all hit or miss, with many huge misses. Even after my discussion with Professor Brown, I often opened the closet at home before heading off to campus, found a mask for the day, wore it, winced, and went home to rummage again in this magic closet. But at least I was conscious of my behavior, and able to calculate, to consider the effects of various masks, to listen to the ways they altered, or helped to embody, my voice.

As a writer who teaches, I have often thought about the parallels between the crafts of writing and teaching. A writer begins with an impulse to create, then casts about for appropriate forms, ways to "give to airy nothings / A local habitation and a name," as Shakespeare put it so memorably in *A Midsummer Night's Dream*. When you first begin to write poems, for example, you tend to sound just like your favorite poets or immediate mentors; this makes perfect sense, given that you learn to write by imitating good writing. Gradually, a poet's voice separates from his or her precursors, becomes distinct, although one can almost always detect the lineage of a poet. When I read the Irish poet Seamus Heaney, for instance, I can hear in every line the harsh, alliterative thrust of the Anglo-Saxon poetry he loves, the "sprung" rhythms of Gerard Manley Hopkins, and the compressed, visionary lyricism of William Butler Yeats. The way he makes use of pastoral imagery recalls the work of Robert Frost, whom Heaney has called a major influence. The mature voice of Heaney has swallowed up, and digested, these precursors; but they remain part of him, ingredients of his own voice. His originality—like the originality of all great artists—is a product of the way he has been able to use what went before him, to absorb and extend a particular tradition, making himself part of it.

The same is true of teaching. You learn to teach by listening closely to your own teachers, by taking on their voices, self-consciously or not, by imitating them, digesting them to the point where they become part of your own voice and persona. You begin as a teacher by imitating *crudely*, moving your arms in familiar ways, pausing in familiar ways, even thinking in familiar ways. This has been vividly true for me. At least half a dozen teachers, from high school through college, served as models. I would imitate one or another on a given day, attempting to fashion a teaching self that seemed true from the bits and pieces of these precursors. Their styles, in fact, were wildly different, so I had to navigate among them. The teaching self that has, over three decades, evolved, is the product of many failed attempts to find the right voice, and many foolish classroom performances. It continues to evolve each semester.

Writers, of course, have always to determine what energy is their own and what derives from other sources. Great writers are like power stations, and it is possible to attach cables to them, to burn on their energy for years. Yeats, for example, lived off William Blake (among others) throughout his life, absorbing his visionary currents, transforming them into his own. But achievement as a writer involves processing these precursors, coming to a point where you are aware of influences and can manage them in such a way that authenticity is no longer the issue. In teaching, you must also come to terms with prior voices, mentors, influences; the long evolution of a particular, and effective, teaching voice involves periods when you are barely in possession of a singular voice, dark days when you question your ability to teach at all. The anxiety of influence affects teachers as well as writers.

Few outside the teaching profession understand the courage it takes to step into a classroom, to wear a mask that you know is a construction, hiding behind it, letting it give shape and substance to your formulations, letting the mask become your face. It takes a certain bravura, even a certain wildness, to let students see you in such a state, at the mercy of a text or inchoate idea, trying to formulate a response to the text, to embody the idea in language that a diverse range of students can assimilate. I always feel a little frightened as I leave my office and begin the long march to the classroom, my arms loaded with notes and texts, my head crammed with ideas I have not quite properly formulated. I wonder what the hell will happen when the class begins. Will I make sense? Will the students respond in sympathetic ways? Will I look and sound like an idiot? Is my face well shaved? Is my fly unzipped? Will I make it through 50 or 60 minutes without feeling like a complete fool?

My guess is that I will keep teaching as long as these questions arise. The fact that I'm asking them means I'm still shaping my teaching persona, still trying to find the right way to present the material, still interested in the kind of communication that teaching involves. I'm still working to create a face, or faces, that will prove useful, true, and distinct. My magic closet is now full of masks; some fit well, others don't. Nevertheless, I'm a little less frightened by the variety in there than I once was, and perhaps a little more willing to play with the mask in front of the class, wiggle it free, peek around its fiery shield.

BY THEIR CLOTHES YE SHALL KNOW THEM:
ON ACADEMIC DRESS

Long after we've forgotten what our professors told us in college, we remember their clothes. Clothes have their own syntax and vocabularies, and they say both more and less than seems apparent. I remember, for example, the impression one English professor made on me during my freshman year in college: he wore frayed and faded jeans to class, with a blue work shirt, the kind a man on the factory line might wear. On his feet were a pair of battered sneakers. It was a look that, at first, startled and excited me. Here, I thought, was a rebel. He identified consciously with the workers of the world, as the shirt suggested. He was somehow beyond the petty, implicit dress codes that governed his colleagues, who (in the late sixties) still wore jackets and ties every day.

I also noticed that this particular professor always managed to find the countermeasures in any text, isolating the ways that authors undermined authority in their work, sometimes unconsciously. (This was deconstruction before Deconstruction.) I think the style of dress he affected worked, in rather subtle ways, to reinforce the method of his teaching. I couldn't see him teaching in the same fashion in a pinstriped, three-piece suit.

Another teacher, an historian, also caught my attention. He invariably wore an expensive suit with a matching vest. A gold watch chain was draped across his stomach, and his shirts were white and heavily starched, with old-fashioned collars that seemed to come straight from the previous century. His leather shoes looked hand-made. A scholar of American history, he seemed to have issued from an earlier period, when gentlemen were gentlemen. He spoke with an easy authority about the past, and represented (to me, at 18) the establishment at its best. He once invited me to his house for tea, and I remember seeing a picture of Benjamin Franklin on the wall. "Ah, Franklin," he said, when I asked about it. "He was my wife's distant relation." Somehow, it didn't surprise me, since he seemed to speak of the American Revolution as a family squabble.

Wishing to become a professor myself one day, I became a close reader of academic clothing. What my teachers wore seemed to suggest a good deal about their scholarly approaches and ideological affiliations, about their cast of mind. Half consciously, I learned to tailor my own prose (in papers and exams) to approximate their fashions. Professor Bluejeans would approve a paper that began something like this: "Walt Whitman sang his own body electric, exploring the world with his own tongue and fingers, sinking them into the sensual crevices of reality." Professor Three-Piece might prefer something along these lines: "The foundations of American democracy were laid by a vigorous mercantile class, who naturally resisted all attempts to impose limits on what struck them as their inalienable right to free trade." As with all writing, the author must know his audience.

Students tend, consciously or not, to respond to the expectations of their teachers, and these expectations often have an ideological coloration. By definition, students are living in an experimental phase of their lives, trying on a pose, an ideology, a stance toward the world as they shift from professor to professor, from discipline to discipline. With luck, they find certain attitudes and habits of thought comfortable and others not; eventually, they develop a manner and style of their own, assembled from the haberdashery of their education. (It's a fairly crude metaphor, I know; but there is plenty of literal truth here to explore.)

When I shifted from a small college in Pennsylvania to the University of St. Andrews, in Scotland, I found my ability to read the dress of my teachers severely challenged. The British class system played havoc with my notions of appropriate dress, but in due course I began to understand the sartorial texts before me, in tutorials and in large lectures. While most lecturers (as in the United States, my college teachers were almost all men) clung to traditional notions of dress, a few were clearly at odds with the system or identified with opposition to the system in some form, and it showed in subtle differences of clothing.

My tutor in British history was an older man who identified with the labor movement. A member of the Fabian Society, a group of left-leaning activists and pamphleteers that famously included Bernard Shaw among their company, he had come to university teaching through the army and Oxford. In dress, he was never going to stray far from the traditional tweed jacket. Indeed, his sartorial rebellions were slight: he wore jeans, for example, when giving tutorials. His shirts were frayed at the cuff and collar, and his ties were a colorful memorial to hundreds of splattered meals. The jackets themselves, made of tweed that resembled strands of iron, not wool, looked indestructible: like a coat of mail. I remember his once saying he had picked up one jacket at Oxfam, in Oxford. "It was about 20 years old," he guessed, with some pride. His preference for solid but very used clothing seemed to cry out something like this: *I am not giving in to fashion. I represent old-fashioned virtues, and consumerism isn't one of them.*

There was another version of this style of dress, although it came from the other side of the political spectrum. My tutor in Medieval History wore iron tweed jackets as well, but his ties defiantly shouted affiliations with various old schools and colleges. (That over 30 years later I remember that he attended Harrow and Trinity College, Cambridge, suggests that it mattered to him, and that he let me know his academic pedigree.) He owned the most solidly built shoes I had ever seen: richly polished brogues. His trousers were corduroy of the old school: hugely ridged, auburn or deep green in color; they were pleated in the front, making them bulge in ways that one might consider embarrassing or fetching, depending on the situation. He often wore a bright, checkered vest under the tweed jackets. On his pinky was a gold signet ring: the sign that he came from a family of some distinction, real or imagined. One would have defined his accent as "plummy." During my years in Britain, I met any number of lecturers who fit this model.

I recall fondly a photograph of Bertrand Russell—a hero of mine—that I kept over my bed in St. Andrews. In it, the great philosopher (also a peer of the realm), wore one of those heavy English suits that declare a certain belief in tradition: a three-piece navy blue suit with bold chalk stripes that seemed to recall the prison bars that Russell had endured for his pacifism during the First World War. That he was a leading voice of the political left (arrested for protesting against the nuclear bomb well into his nineties) seemed less important than his traditional ties to British society, as broadcast by that hand-tailored suit. I always felt it was savvy of Russell to speak his outsider views from the inside, from inside the House of Lords as well as from inside that lordly suit. In a sense, that suit was a piece of battle armor or a kind of sartorial Trojan horse.

In the early seventies, I attended lectures by Sir Isaiah Berlin, the intellectual historian, author of *Four Essays on Liberty* and a subtle study of Karl Marx. He, like Russell, favored traditional pinstriped or dark suits. I noticed that his formal black shoes were always polished to a high sheen. He liked elegant silk ties, too: purple and wine-colored ones, with bold diagonal stripes. Coming from a family of Jewish immigrants, his place in the pecking order of British society was, at least during his earlier years, unstable, although he eventually became a pillar of the establishment: a fellow of All Souls and the British Academy. His suits were, to a degree, defensive, a way of saying that he was surely a member of that establishment, despite his Jewish origins. Though he identified himself as a liberal, he rarely (unlike Russell) dissented in a public way from what might be called normative opinion. What his clothes signaled was a strong desire to be regarded as a man of position, someone whose authority was based on his classical education, his fine intelligence, and his genuine intellectual achievements; they also linked him, via pinstripe, to the city: a world of bankers and lawyers, high civil servants, and members of Parliament.

Living in the United Kingdom, I soon realized that the British appreciate and encourage eccentricity of all kinds, and this was reflected in the dress of dons. I remember several who looked like the male equivalent of bag ladies, though they vaguely adhered to the jacket-and-tie tradition. Their clothes were unkempt and smelly, food stained, and ill fitting. One man in particular would stuff his pockets full of olives at cocktail parties, pulling them out one by one during tutorials, munching on the fuzzy balls unconsciously as he chatted about Keats or Shelley. There was no particular political statement here that I could read. Indeed, I still have difficulty understanding what exactly this disheveled look says to the world apart from something like: *I am an intellectual, deeply concerned with serious matters, and fashion bores me. It is not for serious people.*

Perhaps the most poorly dressed academic I knew was the novelist Iris Murdoch. She had been, for many years, a fellow of an Oxford college, teaching philosophy. She abandoned teaching altogether at one point, but remained in Oxford, married to a professor; she often had dinner at my house, and invariably came looking disheveled, in a heavy wool skirt and baggy pullover. One always saw her walking along the streets of North Oxford in her bag-lady outfit: the gray overcoat that barely skirted the pavement, the odd, lopsided hat; the heavy purse, which might have contained a bowling ball, given the way she carried it. Iris, of course, was a novelist, and her style of dress was an adventure in otherworldliness, an effortless effort to seem effortless. I noticed that a lot of female academics, in Oxford and other academic villages, dressed in quite similar ways.

Indeed, I had a tutor in St. Andrews, a woman, who became a good friend. She wore the baggy wool skirt, the rumpled sweater, the peculiar hat, every day of her life. The only difference between her and Iris Murdoch was the lipstick: a candy-red horizontal stripe across her face that she doubtless considered fetching in some way. It was a signal that she was not married, perhaps; that is, she was available. There was, in her lecturing, a kind of sauciness, a general "come-hither" quality that seemed strangely out of keeping with the context and, in fact, the person. I was not surprised to hear that she died unmarried.

One of the central issues of academic dress for men has always been the tie, or lack of a tie. An absence of ties was noticeable in the late sixties and early seventies among certain kinds of lecturers in British institutions. One of the most gifted literary critics of the middle decades of the twentieth century—F. R. Leavis—was famous for refusing to wear a tie at Cambridge University, where he taught throughout the thirties, forties, fifties, and sixties. He identified with the political Left as one might expect of a tieless man in those days; yet he wanted also to stand apart from the mob. An avid supporter of the Labour Party, he was also a ruthless intellectual snob who turned his nose up at popular culture. I still remember the effect of his dust-jacket photographs on me: the fierce gaze, the open collar, the high forehead crammed with thoughts. His isolation at the peak of British intellectual life seemed, in a lesser way, to echo that of another Cambridge figure: Ludwig Wittgenstein. His casual dress—no tie, of course—combined with an austerity of manner that frightened and intimidated a whole generation of students.

When in the midseventies I came back to the United States to assume a teaching position at Dartmouth, I had to learn a whole new code for academic dress. Professors, most of whom were still men, often wore leather hiking boots, casual trousers, and plaid shirts made of flannel. One got the sense that, after class, they might well just mow a field or repair a fence. Exceptions to this particular style of dress stand out in memory. I recall one well-known economist who passed underneath my apartment window every morning at eight o'clock sharp, wearing a dark suit, a white shirt, a tie, and carrying an attaché case, as though he were about to attend a corporate board meeting in the city. I also remember a flamboyant fellow who taught Scott Fitzgerald and the literature of the twenties, who glided across the campus in a fluffy raccoon coat. I liked to imagine that he and his wife did the Charleston on weekends, at home.

Finding an appropriate style of classroom dress for myself proved difficult. In the beginning, I missed the world of British academia and wanted to associate myself with the legacy of Russell and Berlin. My first major purchase in the line of clothing was a pinstriped suit with a matching vest. I bought another gray flannel suit, and a supply of white shirts and striped regimental ties. I wore these for about two months, until one day a student asked, without malice, "Professor Parini, why do you always dress like a banker?" Had he missed the allusions to Russell and Berlin? Quietly I jettisoned the suit and bought myself some khakis and a stash of button-down shirts in pale colors. I tipped, briefly, toward the preppie mode that seemed current among a certain element of the faculty: Oxford shirts, blue blazers, khaki pants, penny loafers. But that felt inauthentic as well, as I had never attended Exeter or Groton. (West Scranton High just wasn't a preppie place.) I readjusted, stepping into Levi jeans and casual shirts; I often wore a tweed jacket, but without a tie. That seemed about right, and as innocent of ideology as I could manage at the time.

Several decades later, I find myself shifting among various personae with regard to dress. Sometimes I want to feel my connection to the late sixties, to the radical politics that inspired me as a student. I wear jeans on those days, and sometimes even dig an old blue work shirt from the closet. I also have a few billowing shirts like those worn by Russian peasants, and I wear these whenever I lecture on Walt Whitman, considering them as a kind of teaching aid. Whenever I lecture on T. S. Eliot, I try for a more formal manner of dress. Eliot, after all, was a London publisher by profession, and he favored traditional suits with a bowler hat and rolled umbrella as accessories. Last year when teaching *The Waste Land* I put on an old pinstripe, and it felt right in that context. For the most part, I find myself most comfortable in something from the L. L. Bean catalogue.

To a degree, a professor's academic field dictates his or her style of dress. I've noticed that scientists at Middlebury College, where I now teach, prefer casual clothes—a tie might get singed over the Bunsen burner. They often wear solid boots, protecting their toes against a dropped microscope or gravel pick. Language teachers, especially those with a European connection, seem to think of themselves as walking on the streets of Paris or Rome, even though they are living in a state where the cow population is larger than the human one. They often wear elegant fabrics, cut in a Continental way. The women who teach languages are always dressed extremely well, with lots of silk scarves and finely tailored jackets. Some of them even wear dresses.

In the arts and social sciences, one sees a mixture of tweed, jeans, and casual shirts on the men. The women seem to favor casual suits or combinations of skirt-and-blouse. Sensible shoes are required. Because Middlebury is a rural campus, the style is more casual than anything one might encounter on urban campuses, closer to business activities. The idea of a dress code does not exist here, formally; informally, one can often guess correctly at a person's discipline by his or her style of dress.

Of course, there are departmental modes, often tied in to historical styles. The Department of History at Middlebury, when I first came to the college, was full of men in white shirts and ties. Gradually, the dress code for historians has relaxed; but many of the tenured faculty, even the younger ones, still seem to wear a white shirt, a tie and jacket. This hint of formality probably carried over into their teaching, as well. I doubt that many students will call a professor in a shirt and tie by his first name. "Hey, Jack!" will not echo down the hallways.

Teachers often seem to believe they are invisible in the classroom, but this is impossible, a fantasy. Teaching is, after all, a performance art, and whether or not we want to acknowledge it, we assume a costume of sorts every day of the semester. We send countless messages, explicit and implicit, to our students, who are reading us as closely as they read their texts; they (semiconsciously, I suspect) can find clues to our attitudes toward the world as well as our academic subject in the styles we assume, and they will often respond in kind—in their own clothing, and in the ways of thinking manifested in papers and exams. As a college teacher, it pays to think of clothing as a rhetorical choice, and to dress accordingly.

ROBERT FROST AS EXAMPLE

Gore Vidal once said to me that teaching has ruined more writers than alcohol. I never really agreed with him on this, believing in my gut that it is not only possible but advisable for a writer—or some kinds of writers, I should say—to teach. A teacher spends a lot of time assimilating new material, then thinking of ways to make this material available to students. The work involves clarification, classification, and persuasion: the art of rhetoric. In this regard, teaching and good writing go hand in hand, reinforcing each other.

Having written a biography of Robert Frost, I've come to understand a little better what it means for a writer to teach, and how a writer's teaching might benefit students and the writer as well. Frost had experience as a teacher at every level, beginning at the age of 18, when he dropped out of Dartmouth to take over his mother's elementary school class in Methuen, Massachusetts. His mother, whose nerves were weak, was driven away from the classroom by unruly sixth and seventh graders, who called her names and refused to do any work. Fights—with flying fists—often broke out during lessons. More than once a piece of fruit splattered on her blackboard as she attempted to write on it.

Frost saw at once that the kids needed a firm hand. His first move was to buy a rattan cane from the local hardware store; he propped it on his desk in full view of the class, prepared to argue the point *ad baculum*. They settled down quickly, getting back to their work with remarkably little fuss. A school board report at the Methuen annual town meeting that year put the matter succinctly: "Mr. Frost, although young, bears an unusual record for scholarship and maturity of character and has shown marked success in the management and instruction of a difficult school." He was praised for his "old-fashioned approach."

Frost continued to teach at the elementary level, off and on, for several years, always with success. But after he married, in 1895, he returned to college, attending Harvard for a couple of years before dropping out once again. This time, he decided on agriculture instead of teaching as an appropriate career, and he bought a chicken farm in Derry, New Hampshire, with the help of his paternal grandfather. There was no real money in this, of course; Frost lived the life of subsistence farmers, barely able to put food on the table. In 1906, with four children to support, he took a part-time job in the English Department at Pinkerton Academy, a local high school, in order to supplement his income. This soon became a full-time job, and Frost began to cultivate a teaching persona that he would experiment with and develop over the next six decades.

He was, recalled one Pinkerton student, "an eccentric but vivid teacher" who usually entered the classroom "at a gallop." In class, Mr. Frost would "slump down in his chair behind his desk, almost disappearing from sight except for his heavy-lidded eyes and bushy brows. In such a position, he would talk, or he might read aloud or let a discussion go its own length. Other teachers didn't know how to take him, and students accustomed to prepared lessons were inclined to think they could take advantage of a teacher who was not strict in the way they knew." Clearly, Frost had abandoned the rattan cane, preferring a self-presentation more suited to students at a higher level.

He remained at Pinkerton until the principal there, Ernest Silver, resigned to take up a job as president of the New Hampshire State Normal School in Plymouth. Frost had built up such a reputation among the students at Pinkerton that he was invited by Silver to join the faculty in Plymouth, even though he had no college degree. He began, even more energetically, to develop a classroom manner that was characterized by students as witty, playful, and teasing. He confronted students boldly, forcing them to face their own prejudices. "The class was just one long, wild conversation," one student at Plymouth remembered. "Frost made some of us uncomfortable, forcing us to look at subjects honestly and address them in our own voice, but we admired him."

The Plymouth job, however, lasted only a year. Frost inherited a sum of money from his grandfather, and he decided to take his family to England, where he and his wife had always wanted to "live under thatch." He was now in his midthirties, and had yet to publish much of anything. At Plymouth, he had felt the tug familiar to all writers who teach, with the classroom pulling one way, the writing desk another. Both are demanding, and both enticing. He decided to take the plunge, to see what he could really make of himself as a poet.

Three years later, he returned to America with two books in print, and a small but rapidly expanding reputation. He bought a small farm in Franconia, New Hampshire, having managed to preserve much of the capital from the sale of the previous farm. Now he settled into a routine of farming and writing: always an agreeable combination for him. But the classroom beckoned again in the summer of 1916, when Alexander Meiklejohn, the innovative young president of Amherst College, paid him an unexpected call. Frost was invited to teach for the spring semester of 1917. Meiklejohn believed, quite rightly, that there was plenty of room for a poet on the faculty—someone who could present an example of the writing life to students, and someone who could teach writing from the inside, as a working writer.

Frost listened attentively to Meiklejohn, and liked what he heard. He took the job, on the condition that he would have plenty of time to write. As it turned out, Frost proved an able and inspiring teacher, known to generations of Amherst students. Indeed, Frost would be associated with Amherst, as faculty member or occasional poet-in-residence, until his death in 1963. He would also teach for intervals at the University of Michigan, Dartmouth, Harvard, and Middlebury. "I'm a farmer and poet and teacher," he wrote in his journal in 1920, "and I'm all three at once." In a way, these three avocations dovetailed nicely, with each role informing and reinforcing the others.

Frost was always, however, an eccentric teacher, somewhat at odds with the culture of the academy. "I hate academic ways," he told one interviewer. "I fight everything academic. Think of what time we waste in trying to learn academically—and what talent we staunch with academic teaching." Presumably by "academic teaching" he meant teaching that was dead on its feet, uninformed by the give-and-take of the mind at play. He disliked rote learning, and he was mistrustful of "content" as the goal of education. He did not believe that the specific texts a student was given to study mattered very much; what counted, he wrote in his journal, was that "students are made to think fresh and fine, to stand by themselves, to make a case."

He believed in what he called "teaching by presence" and repeatedly suggested that informal contacts between teachers and students were vastly more important than anything that happened inside the classroom walls. But within the classroom, too, he sought the freedom of informal contact: "It is the essence of symposium I am after," he said. "Heaps of ideas and the subject matter of books [are] purely incidental." He once told a class at Amherst: "I'm looking for subject matter, for substance, in yourself." And in his journal in 1917, he wrote: "What we do in college is to get over our little-mindedness. To get an education you have to hang around till you catch on." Frost understood what I suspect all great teachers know instinctively, that *tone* is everything in the classroom: the attitude of the teacher toward the material. This tone is the unique gift of the teacher to the student, and it is what students recall long after the specific subject matter has faded from memory.

As might be expected, not every student responded warmly to Frost's methods. "Mr. Frost's was the most loosely run and undisciplined class of any of the classes I attended in college," one student from Amherst complained. Another said Frost was "headstrong with his own ideas" and was "so involved with his own thinking that there was no room for discussion." Early in his teaching career, a rude handful of Amherst students actually played cards at the back of the classroom while Frost talked, although he seemed (or pretended to be) oblivious to their distractions.

In 1976, I interviewed John Dickey, who was president of Dartmouth when Frost taught there in the 1940s. He recalled that "Frost came into one class early in the term and asked the students, who had just written their first paper, if anybody had written anything that they could stand by passionately. When nobody raised a hand, he promptly threw all the papers into the waste basket and left the room, telling them to come back next time with something they *could* stand by passionately." In this age of consumer-driven education, when teachers are often terrified of student evaluations (upon which their careers depend), one can hardly imagine such a scene taking place, however instructive.

Dickey said to me, "Frost's wildness, his vitality, struck anyone who took his courses. His low, rumbling voice lingered over each word, with frequent pauses followed by repetitions of phrases and notions. He didn't really teach a subject so much as teach himself, his way of thinking and being in the world. His mind, his conversation, ranged widely over everything from literature to politics to sports, but he had a way of making connections, of stitching together disparate things." Frost was, in other words, an artist in the classroom, creating new wholes from matter not previously thought related.

One of the best of many descriptions of what Frost was like in the classroom is by Charles W. Cole, a future president of Amherst who recalled a visit to his German literature class by Frost in the 1920s: "Frost began to discuss metaphors in an easy way, asking occasional questions to bring out our ideas. Gradually the evening shadows lengthened and after a while Frost alone was talking. The room grew darker and darker until we could not see each others' faces. But no one even thought of turning on the light. The dinner hour came and went, and still no one of that half score of hungry boys dreamed of leaving. We dared not even stir for fear of interrupting. Finally, long after seven, Frost stopped and said, 'Well, I guess that's enough.' We thanked him and left as if under a spell." Can one imagine a better class?

I often feel that the wildness has gone out of teaching, a wildness that pushes students to question basic assumptions, about themselves and the world. It is much safer to rely on "content," to believe that if students have studied a certain sequence of texts, have taken notes and sat exams on this material, that they have somehow moved closer to being educated. In truth, it is having a stance toward this material, a tone, a manner of address, that matters more. From what I have gathered in talking to many of his former students, Frost gave the class something they could take with them out into the world after they left college: an approach to reading and thinking that was radically skeptical of the text and its rhetoric. He gave them a way of being in the world, too, that involved making endless connections, of drawing things into comparison. He taught them, most importantly, about metaphor, which he saw lying at the heart of the human intellectual enterprise.

In his famous essay, "Education by Poetry," Frost wrote: "Poetry begins in trivial metaphors, pretty metaphors, 'grace' metaphors, and goes on to the profoundest thinking that we have.

Poetry provides the one permissible way of saying one thing and meaning another." He cautioned that "unless you have had your proper poetic education in the metaphor, you are not safe anywhere. Because you are not at ease with figurative values: you don't know the metaphor in its strength and its weakness. You don't know how far you may expect to ride it and when it may break down with you. You are not safe in science; you are not safe in history."

As both teacher and writer (and probably farmer as well), Frost put an emphasis on metaphor and analogical thinking. In this, his roles converged beautifully. Being a teacher, he had an opportunity to think aloud with students, to enter into conversations that tested, and developed, his own range of intellectual play. He learned, in teaching, how to ride out a metaphor, and what to expect from it. He learned when it would break down, when he had to withdraw from it. This knowledge was doubtless carried over into his poetry, where metaphorical thinking takes center stage.

In my own teaching, I have tried to cultivate this wildness, to keep the class on edge, wondering what I will do next, what I will say. I take risks, and this means I sometimes fail miserably, saying idiotic things; but these risks have been worth taking. The classroom, for me, can become a place where sparks fly, where students confront their own best selves, thinking aloud, with me or against me, as we move toward something like Truth. When I see or feel myself growing tame, or conventional, or boring, I think of Frost, and I try to get something of that unpredictability and risk into my performance.

GETTING THINGS DONE

I don't care what they say: it *is* possible to write and teach at the same time. In fact, I have a hard time writing without teaching. (Sabbaticals are always disastrous interludes for me, a time when I tend to sink into depression, writing more slowly, thinking a lot less clearly.) Teaching organizes my life, gives a structure to my week, puts before me certain goals: classes to conduct, books to reread, papers to grade, meetings to attend. I move from event to event, having a clear picture in my head of what I must do next. Without the academic calendar in front of me, I feel lost.

I've been teaching for several decades, and in that time I've written and edited a lot of stuff, including novels and volumes of poetry, biographies, essays, and reviews. I'm saying this not to brag. I'm too old for that, and I don't confuse quantity with quality. (I often point out to students that Chidiok Tichborne wrote only one poem that anybody knows, an elegy for himself, composed as he waited to be executed for treason against Queen Elizabeth I. It is worth a shelf of books by most other poets.) I simply want to make the point that I like being productive, enjoy writing, and have never found myself without the time to write, even when large numbers of students required my attention. I should add that where I work there are no graduate students waiting in the wings to grade my papers or conduct discussion sessions.

There is, nevertheless, a certain spectacle in overproduction. I've been fascinated by people like Harold Bloom, who can turn out large and complicated books year after year for many decades without seeming to tire. There is an old joke, doubtless apocryphal, that runs something like this: A student calls at the front door of Professor Bloom's house in New Haven. He asks to see Professor Bloom. "I'm sorry," says Mrs. Bloom, "but Harold is writing a book." "That's all right," replies the student, "I can wait."

Versions of this story circulate through the literary and academic world. Among writers, I look on Joyce Carol Oates, John Updike, Gore Vidal, and others, with amazement, wondering how they do it. Their books arrive in stores, neatly packaged, copy-edited and blurbed, with the predictability of the seasons themselves. Once again: productivity does not substitute for quality. But one does look at such prolific writers and scholars with incredulity. How do they do it? Are they teaching as well as writing? Don't they have committee meetings to attend? Do they have an army of research assistants helping them? Should they sign their names, "School of So-and-So," since they merely supervise the production line?

As a graduate student in St. Andrews, I watched a few of my more prolific mentors carefully. One of them, an extremely productive and original scholar of Greek literature, culture, and language, was Sir Kenneth Dover. His books on Aristophanic comedy, Greek homosexuality, and Greek syntax, have proven seminal works. His writing is meticulously researched, thoughtful, and written with clarity and argumentative force. He personally ran the Department of Greek, and had large responsibilities around the university. I once asked him the secret of his productivity and he said, without hesitation: "I've learned how to use the odd gaps of 20 minutes or so that occur at various points in the day."

Most of us—myself included—waste vast amounts of time. I don't actually mind that, I should add. Like Robert Frost, I believe that laziness is essential to creativity; I get a lot done because I have time to burn. I tell myself over and over that there is so much time, so little to do. This means that I feel rather free, unconstrained, and eager to work when I feel like working. I have learned, like Sir Kenneth, to make use of little pockets of time: the half hour before dinner, for example, when the food is cooking. This stretch can be very productive. Weekends are full of time, even when a lot of chores have to be accomplished. I suspect that most of us fail to use the hours of the day properly. We imagine, foolishly, that huge quantities of time are needed to settle into a project, to reactivate the engines of thought.

Most good work gets done in short stretches. It isn't really possible to concentrate for more than half an hour without a solid break. That is my experience, in any case. Even when I have the whole day to work, I stop every 20 minutes to make a cup of tea, eat a cookie, call a friend, do a little yoga or a few stomach crunches, shower, or take a short walk. At a certain point in my life I realized that I should not feel guilty about taking these breaks. I try not to feel guilty about anything, even when I am guilty.

Of course it helps to have writing time you can count on. I have gone to a village diner in Middlebury for breakfast at roughly 8:10 almost every morning for several decades. During that hour or so, over coffee and English muffins (with peanut butter), I write poems. Rough drafts, mostly. I have grown used to the chatter in the background, the easy flow of coffee, the local crowd coming in and out. I know most of the people who come into the diner. Many of them wave, nod, or speak to me briefly. A few will sit down for a few minutes. But they all know I'm working. My notebook is open. I have a pen in my hand. I've made it known in these parts that I write poetry at this diner in the morning, and my friends (and acquaintances) respect that.

A little work every day adds up. That was a concept I got from John Updike, whom I heard say (many years ago, in some public forum) that he only writes two pages a day. Two pages a day adds up to a long book every year, even counting revisions. When I'm working on a large prose book, such as a novel or biography, I try to write two pages or so every day. I'm not neurotic about it:

sometimes you don't feel like writing any pages. But I aim for two, and I usually get two. The system works. (And, like Hemingway, I always stop at a point where I know what comes next; that makes getting into the material easier the next day.)

Updike apparently compartmentalizes his writing life. Living in a big house on the North Shore (of Massachusetts), he is lucky enough to have several studies: one for fiction, one for reviews and nonfiction, one for letters and business. He can move along the hall, stopping in for a certain amount of time with a novel, working on a review for a time, an essay for a time, perhaps a poem or short story for another chunk of time. He has never taught, of course, so he can move easily among writing projects, at will. It sounds nice.

I would get bored, however, without my teaching. I need contact with students and colleagues, the sense of community. I like the demands of preparation for a class: rereading a favorite poet or novelist, skimming a recent critical article. I am afraid that, if left to my own devices, I might not reread Stevens, Frost, Eliot, Yeats, and other poets in a systematic fashion, year after year. And these poets have sustained me, provided spiritual refreshment, furnished the rooms of my mind with decent stuff. I find it very useful to put my thinking about their poetry into words in front of a class.

Kenneth Dover also told me that teaching would serve me well in this way; he once suggested to me that a class and a critical essay are very similar in that each requires powers of formulation; each draws on the analytical intelligence. It was T. S. Eliot who said that criticism is as natural as breathing, and I believe that. When I read something, I want to talk about it. I want to compare it to other texts. I want to match my own voice with the voice of the text. This is what it means to be a thinking person.

I keep at least two or three projects on the boil at any given time. This means I am never at a loss for something urgent to accomplish. I can always turn from a poem to a novel, a book review, an essay. Each genre has its different demands, and I have come to relish the differences; an idea always has its perfect form, but it may take several attempts to find that form. I've taken the same notion and tried to embody it as a poem, then as a story, then as an essay. One can, of course, adapt a notion from one form to another; but I do believe in the ideal form for each idea; I do try to find that form.

Teaching, too, calls upon us to move in many directions. There is always a class to prepare, a book to read or read again, a paper to grade, a meeting to attend. I have never in 30 years not had a letter of recommendation urgently waiting to be written. Moving among these tasks, I try to make haste slowly, stopping wherever I am to focus, to give whatever I have to give at that moment. I think I've actually learned this by writing, by having to stare at the page in front of me, the line of poetry breaking at the moment, spilling over onto the next line, the essay in need of a final twist. It is always better to work in small bursts, to focus on the twist or turn ahead.

Having a grand idea, and setting up to accomplish something in a grand way, has always been, for me, a hopeless notion. I once had a good friend, a poetry editor and teacher, who always hoped to write a novel. One day, the first sentence of the novel swam into his head: "All of Malaysia was agog." He didn't know why they were agog, or even where on earth Malaysia was. But he applied for a grant, got it, and set himself up in a foreign country with a huge sheaf of paper and a typewriter. He typed with reverence the great first sentence. He waited. He waited for much of a year, but nothing ever came. In those circumstances, of course, it never would.

THE EMERITUS PROFESSOR

"That is no country for old men," Yeats once wrote. The same might be said of the United States in the twenty-first century. Old men and women are cast aside, left to bide their time in retirement villages or campers. The lucky ones retain their health, living independently of their children, chopping wood or building model airplanes or filling in the blanks of their lives with some analogous activity. It's a sorry fate, and one that should not, it seems, befall academics.

We are lucky folks, in that we like our jobs; indeed, we have that miraculous thing, a vocation that is also an avocation. In theory, when we retire, we simply move to another phase—the research phase, if you will—of our careers, a kind of permanent Guggenheim leading up to those golden open stacks overhead, in heaven. The problem is, it rarely turns out that way.

Over several decades of teaching, I've become attached to many older colleagues, only to see them disappear after their final graduation, the dubious badge of emeritus pinned to their gowns. But there is no merit in emeritus, not in most American colleges or universities. Emeritus means goodbye, *hasta la vista*. The familiar faces are suddenly absent from department meetings. They no longer pace the hallway, answer the phone, or offer candid words of advice. Students quickly forget their names. Former colleagues barely seem to recall their presence. Then younger colleagues come on board, and they have never even heard of Professor So-and-So, once so popular with students, once a respected scholar in the field. If one catches sight of this emeritus professor, in the library or at some concert in the college chapel, there is merely a furtive, rather guilty, nod of acknowledgement. *You should be dead by now,* we appear to say to them. And this is despicable.

That emeritus faculty can play a crucial role in the lives of younger colleagues was, by chance, made evident to me as a young instructor. During my first term at Dartmouth, a retired professor called Maurice Quinlan stopped by my office in the basement of Sanborn House. Maury was a friend of a friend, and he had once taught at Dartmouth, too—40 years or so before me. He had moved around a lot, ending his career at Boston College; he was a distinguished teacher and the author of several well-regarded books on eighteenth-century literature. After retiring, he moved to a small house near Dartmouth, having had fond memories of his early days of teaching there. He used the college library most days, working on scholarly projects to the end. A lifelong bachelor, he retained a lively wit and immense geniality into his eighties.

We became good friends, and I found myself increasingly eager for his guidance. I would take my syllabus to him before each term began, looking for advice, and it was always first-class advice. He knew what worked and what didn't. Once I revised a syllabus three times under his direction—much to the benefit of my students. He and I would discuss books that might well go onto the syllabus and discuss the best approaches to certain difficult texts. Once or twice he sat in on my classes, offering comments that proved remarkably helpful. Of course Maury would never vote on my tenure. He would never offer an official word on my behalf. So this was mentoring in the purest sense.

There was nothing I couldn't discuss with Maury, personal or professional, and our weekly lunches at the Hanover Inn became a prized ritual. He learned from me about the painful abrasions of departmental politics at Dartmouth, and he heard about my constant frustration in trying to balance the demands of teaching and scholarship—no easy trick for anyone, but especially hard on young teachers, who are new to everything. In one time of severe personal crisis, I sought out Maury in something like desperation; he listened to me closely, and was kind, wise, and stern in his response. The severity of his approach was essential: he had experienced some versions of my situation, and he seemed to know exactly what I should do. You cannot buy that kind of counsel.

I had been to see Maury only a few weeks before he died. It so happened that I had sent him a manuscript of an article I was writing only a few weeks before, and—in his typically generous manner—he had marked it up. "I'm afraid I've scratched out quite a bit," he said. That was an understatement. He had scratched out most of it, and most of it deserved cancellation. But the parts that remained were underlined boldly, with "good" written in the margins here and there. In several places he had written "develop" or "expand." I knew instinctively what he meant by those cryptic commands, since we had had conversations along these lines before. The pity was they could not continue.

My point should be obvious by now. The retired professor holds a great treasure in his or her palms: experience. It's the kind of thing that only trial and error can produce. The institutional memory that old heads carry is desperately needed by younger faculty members, who should not have to reinvent the wheel at every meeting, at the beginning of every term. Forgetting is the easiest thing in the world to do, and the hardest thing to recover from. So it's not mere kindness to "include" emeriti in the workings of an institution. It is common sense.

In 1993–1994, I spent a year at Christ Church College, Oxford, as a visiting fellow, and I was struck by the wisdom of their attitude to retired faculty. The difference between those "on staff" and those "formerly on staff" appeared rather slight. Retired fellows often came into lunch, and were fully conversant with the politics of the college, with teaching issues, with the scholarship of their younger colleagues, which they seemed ready and willing to discuss. They had pride of place at high table in the main dining hall each evening. One of my favorite colleagues was a retired scientist, a lovely man in his late seventies, who spent all day in the lab and rarely missed a lunch in college. He still helped postgraduate students, as needed, and taught the occasional seminar in biochemistry. He traveled the world to attend conferences. He was working on several important projects. He still is, as far as I know.

I don't see why this model should not work in American institutions, and the expense would be just the sort of thing alumni might enjoy subsidizing, since we are talking about *their* former teachers. Ideally, scientists would retain full access to labs and research facilities. And retired professors should, if they wish to do so, retain an office in their given department—not in some game preserve on the edge of campus for hoary-headed creatures. They should have access to the same secretarial help and professional development funds that were always available to them. They should be invited to attend faculty and department meetings, be encouraged to teach on a regular basis, and be asked to advise students in their special areas of interest. More to the point, they should be respected for what they are: honored citizens in a community of scholars.

I'm aware that resources are often scant, and that financing the professional lives of retirees is not every institution's idea of an essential activity. But I am suggesting that this expense would not be superfluous, and that active faculty might actually benefit from the help of old hands. As ever, each institution will have to consider its priorities carefully, without overlooking this one. There can be, I suspect, a good deal of bang for the buck here, as emeritus professors draw no salary and, in fact, might want to contribute to fund-raising efforts among their former students. There could be quite explicit arrangements by which emeriti professors are regularly called upon to meet with alumni, tying their office space and use of facilities to their willingness to continue functioning within the community in some capacity.

Many retired professors will, undoubtedly, choose separation and forgetting; they will retreat to southern Florida in their campers and occupy themselves with golf and casual reading, or live abroad by the sea, sipping wine as they read their way through foreign newspapers; but that scenario might change over time, as institutions opened themselves to the benefits that would accrue from making the rank of emeritus professor a meaningful one. The energy for effecting this change would have to come from both sides of the retirement line, as the institutions made the appropriate gestures, and as they in turn were reciprocated by emeritus faculty, who would have to make the appropriate commitments—to teaching and scholarship. Of course the commitment to scholarship would necessarily be primary for emeriti.

The cult of youth in the United States has clearly damaged the academy. Especially in the humanities, excellence in scholarship often demands decades of preparation and immense patience. Young scholars in search of tenure and grants are too often encouraged to publish immature work—work naively absorbed in whatever disciplinary approaches and their accompanying jargon happen to be fashionable. The ancient symbol of the revered, old scholar—full of wisdom and years, with a shrewd, ironic, generous perspective on the field—seems lost in time, although a few examples of the kind exist.

I knew one man who, during 50 years of teaching, published very little. He was a teacher's teacher, committed to the classroom in admirable ways, always eager to meet with students in his office to discuss their ideas, to focus on their problems, and to read their work. He was always available to his colleagues, showing an interest in their research, offering suggestions based on his own enormous reading. Because of his lack of publications, he would probably not get tenure in the academy these days. What is fascinating here is that when he finally retired, at 70 or so, he devoted himself to scholarship, publishing several monumental works on Russian literature in his final, fruitful decade. This was scholarship that revealed a well-tempered mind, seasoned by decades of voracious reading in many languages, deepened by experience.

One can, of course, overestimate the benefits of age, which may only serve to confirm prejudice and harden bad habits. But genuine wisdom necessarily involves a refining process that takes time. I've talked to enough retired professors to know that what they have to offer is valuable beyond calculation. The system, in its current form, does not encourage faculty to grow and develop beyond the age of retirement, which means there is little incentive to develop and, as crucially, to refine and utilize the knowledge and intellectual skills acquired over a lifetime. The few who buck the system, who thrive as scholars beyond their last day in the class-room, are exemplary in the widest sense. We should emulate them, revere them, and encourage our institutions to put in place the structural, financial, and emotional supports that will encourage everyone to see—really to see—that emeritus status is a goal worth aiming toward.

Nitty-Gritty

Okay, you've got your first job. I was there, 30 years ago, but—unfortunately—there was nobody around to write me the sort of letter I'm writing to you. I don't even know you, but I feel a certain responsibility, mostly because I want to spare you some of the mistakes I made, to make your life in the classroom, in the academic village, a little easier. Like all advice, you can take it or leave it.

One of the main things I can say to you is that every teacher, like every person, is different. You have to teach out of who you are. That is the only way you will succeed, as a professional, as a teacher and scholar, as a member of the community of scholars. You will have to adapt anything I say here to your own private vision, to some version of yourself. The essential journey in this profession is toward self-knowledge; this will involve getting lost in order to get found, losing your thread, having to revise your sense of reality over and over, frequently adjusting to new information, new contexts. In modeling this revisionary path, you will help your students to learn how to forge their own paths.

I will assume that you went into the teaching profession because you thought you had a gift for teaching or scholarship—or both. You liked a few teachers along the way and you thought you could emulate their success. Perhaps you were just fascinated by the field: literature, physics, whatever. You wanted to spend your life around people fascinated by this field, who take their work in a given subject seriously. You liked, perhaps, the smell of the lab or library, the feel of scholarly journals in your hands. You enjoyed hearing intelligent people argue. That is probably as good a place to begin as anywhere, but you nevertheless have to make your way in the profession: among students and among your colleagues, some of whom will vote on your tenure.

Again I will return to the basic advice: be yourself, but build on that notion, adding to yourself, amplifying yourself. Make your viewpoint known, to students and your colleagues. And don't be afraid to change your mind as needed. "A foolish consistency is the hobgoblin of little minds," said Emerson. I always liked that aphorism; it has given me courage, many times, to shift my opinion.

Let me say right off that I made the mistake of not making my viewpoint known at first. I was shy, frightened, and uncertain about the value of my personal take on various matters, academic and otherwise. I sat quietly, even mutely, in department meetings. I was intimidated by loud colleagues who made their points of view known in ways that upset me. I was somewhat hesitant with students as well. They could get away with saying foolish things in class, or getting things dead wrong, without my objecting. This was all foolish of me. It was a mistake. I wish, in retrospect, I had been able to locate and speak from a clear perspective, risking a point of view.

That may be impossible advice, of course. A clear perspective takes time to develop, and hard work, and much sifting of selves. It takes the spiritual equivalent of meditation, even prayer. The sooner you get going on this, the better. Always ask yourself the basic questions: Why am I doing this? What do I have to say to students about this material? What values do I bring to the profession? Where am I in agreement or disagreement with the prevailing attitudes? Am I afraid to say what I think?

The best thing you can do for yourself, as a young instructor, is to think and speak honestly, registering in an unambiguous way your current position, while cultivating a certain openness to change, to the attitudes and approaches of others. Be respectful of every colleague and every student: listen to them, deeply and truly. But speak your piece when the time comes, letting the chips fall where they may.

Remember that you got your job because somebody thought you were a competent scholar: literary critic, physicist, historian, philosopher. At the beginning stages of your teaching life, you will have few credentials—a doctoral degree, perhaps, a number of small publications. But you are starting out. The main thing is to take the long view: understand that you will gain a foothold in the field, but this takes time and effort. Try to imagine a large trajectory for yourself, as scholar and teacher. Visualize yourself as a senior member of your department, your profession. Think what it meant to get there, and how you got there. I loved making lists of books I might write someday when I was in my twenties. In my late fifties, I am surprised at how many of these books—or books like them—I actually wrote. It is fun to look ahead, to dream, to consider the scope of your life before it unfolds. It helps to head in a certain direction.

There always seem to be those who would rather spend their time in the classroom than in the library. This is problematic in the academic world as it has evolved, especially if you teach at a competitive institution, where standards for publication are fairly high. My hunch is that if you want to spend most of your time in the classroom, thinking about your courses and your students, you had better make sure that you are employed by an institution that values teaching. Many smaller colleges, especially those with a strongly regional clientele, do not demand much in the way of publications for tenure. You have to make sure you understand the real requirements for tenure at your institution, and there is no better way to accomplish this than to ask around, talking mostly to those who have most recently gotten tenure. They will have a pretty good idea of what is required, and will probably welcome a frank discussion along these lines.

You might also ask around to see what sorts of teachers were denied tenure in recent times. I've been around long enough to have seen many fine teachers abandoned by the college where I work because they didn't manage to get a book published in time for their review. They assumed their case would somehow be different. Avoid a nasty surprise and make sure you understand exactly what is required, being aware that all institutions make exceptions. But don't bank on being the exception to the rule, since you probably won't be.

The main thing is that you must take your work—as teacher and scholar—seriously. Hard work is the name of the game, in academic life as elsewhere. You must prepare each course thoughtfully, taking time to write an intelligent, easy-to-follow syllabus. Students hate uncertainty, fuzziness, or a lack of clear goals. Make sure that on your syllabus you let the students know exactly what is required of them: how many papers, how long, when they are due, and so forth. Make sure that midterm and final exams are listed, in bold letters. Then be sure you stick to the syllabus. There is nothing more frustrating to a student than watching a teacher get bogged down, and not moving toward stated goals.

This does not, of course, mean that flexibility isn't important. You may well venture into byways, little excursions that will serve in some way to illustrate a point or, merely, to entertain the students, providing comic relief. This is okay. But get back to the menu as soon as possible. Students do not want to go home without knowing where they have been, without seeing and feeling some accomplishment.

During the first class of any term, tell the students up front what a good grade means, in your view. That is, tell them what they must do to succeed in your course as bluntly as you can. I say something like this to my students: "If you want to get an A in this course, you will have to write papers that demonstrate genuine freshness of thought, even some originality. I want to see that you have engaged a subject in a deep and personal way. The paper must be well organized and free of mechanical errors. It must be well documented and well argued. If you do strong, clear work that nevertheless seems derivative, clichéd, or sloppy, you can still get a B of some kind if the work rises to a decent standard of clarity and intellectual force. B means good, not great. It is, these days, the norm for a reasonably hard-working and honest student. If the paper is poorly organized and somewhat mediocre in its presentation of a fairly obvious argument, you can expect a C of some kind. I reserve D for those who have flaunted their lack of responsibility, presenting work that is truly weak in terms of argument and writing. F is for those who fail to turn in anything resembling a college-level paper—or those who borrow one from the internet." I make that speech several times a year, and I stick to those criteria.

As regards class attendance, you had best figure out where you stand. I spent a good deal of time in a British university, where attendance at lectures was strictly "optional," so I have always had some reluctance to force my own students to attend a large class, especially if the format is that of a lecture. Seminars, however, only work if the class comes, and if everyone gets involved, so I always make it clear that attendance is required. These days, I urge students to attend my lecture courses as well, often teasing them with this line: "I must tell you that I happen to have a photographic memory. After I've called the roll a couple of times, I will know your face, and I will always know if you are present or not. Beware." Ever since I developed that line, I have rarely experienced significant absences.

Needless to say, the best way to get students to come to your classes with a real sense of commitment is to make the classroom a place where good things happen. I like to be extremely open with students, telling them about my personal response to a text, talking about difficulties of reading the text that may be personal or may, of course, be part of the text itself. I never fail to provide a few amusing or startling autobiographical details along the way: students are trying to piece together a vision of their teacher, so you might as well help. I like to make jokes—at my own expense, usually. Once in a while I tease a student about his or her clothing or hairstyle or whatever: this can be done in ways that do not humiliate them but actually make them feel closer to you. I try to keep the class moving forward at a steady pace, and this involves speaking rather more quickly than I would normally do: I find that it actually helps to keep them awake.

I vary my pace as well, sometimes pausing for what can seem like a very long time to students unused to silence in the classroom. Use those silences. Let tension build, then break it swiftly, calling on a student by name, or bringing your fist down on the desk. These methods all seem a bit fake and theatrical, but you must remember that a class is a performance. Almost anything you can do to enhance that performance is permissible.

It can catch the attention of students in useful ways if you occasionally bring visual aids into class or use whatever high-tech tools you have at your disposal, such as computer-generated overheads or clips from videos. I am a low-tech teacher, a real Luddite for the most part, but I have been impressed by colleagues who do employ technology effectively, and have occasionally dabbled in its use. (I still recall a lecturer in Scotland who brandished a Viking sword when reading passages from Icelandic epics. It was comical, but effective in its way. One became vividly aware of what it could mean to have such a sword, as one Old Norse poet put it, "brought down with force upon a bare, warm neck.")

Remember that your job is to demonstrate before students the *process* of thinking. Don't just read a script that you have prepared, verbatim. That is boring—unless you have remarkable reading skills. It's never a good idea to fall asleep during your own lecture. Instead, dance on the high wire of extemporaneous talk. Think about the material at hand, and make that thought apparent and dramatic. Sweat or weep if you can. (I can't.) Agonize in public. (This I can manage.) Make it feel as though you are discovering each thought as though you were Einstein himself stumbling upon the theory of relativity. Remember that you are trying to provide students with the sensation of thinking as well as the thoughts themselves. It's not enough merely to relay the material at hand.

To "perform" in this way without making your teaching an empty vessel that nevertheless gleams, put the time into preparation, and make sure that before each class you have a written set of goals. Ask yourself these questions: What should the student carry away from this class? What specific facts are essential? What attitude toward the material do you wish to convey? What questions might students have that you can answer? How can you make them eager to expand their knowledge of a given subject?

Since I teach literary subjects, I have the advantage of working from a given text. That text remains at the center of each class, and I love reading from it aloud. I dramatize the adventure of the text, the sound of its sense, the physical texture of its being. I try to focus on transitional moments, difficult points. I'm also aware of the silence around the words, the absences built into the presences of the writing. I often talk about why this text is, or is not, regarded as canonical. I locate its political situation, its situation in the culture at large. I never hesitate to refer to parallel texts, works that may relate to this text found in popular culture: television shows, films, magazines, the world of sports. I impress upon students that every text is written by a man or woman lodged in a specific life and specific times. What are the relevant facts, then? How do these facts relate to the text itself? These things interest students, who are living their own lives, in their own times, and wondering how to react to them.

I wish that, when I began teaching, I had viscerally understood that teaching and scholarship are integrally related, and that they reinforce each other; there should not be a separation between the two. But I wish I had understood also that teachers must, and usually do, make their own peace with the profession, and that it is never wise to make judgments about one's colleagues. The old biblical saying, "Judge not, lest ye be judged," still holds. You will, of course, be judged by your senior colleagues at various stages in the game; they will assess your teaching and your scholarship as well as your contribution to the community. But there is no point in trying to assess *them*, unless you are specifically asked to do so. Generosity is always the best approach.

As for the old saw, publish or perish, you must look around and figure out what is sufficient for your institution. An article or two may do. Or you may need to publish two books for tenure. Either way, you must know your situation and make sure that, whatever else happens, you get tenure. I didn't, the first time around, and it made my life hell for a few years. Don't let that happen to you. Pay close attention to your teaching, and develop a routine that allows you to do your research and writing. The great blessing of academic jobs is that there is always enough time for both of these activities—at most institutions. If you happen to be teaching somewhere where the teaching load is especially high, the chances are that the demands on your time for scholarship will be less.

That is all right, if you should wish to stay at that institution or a similar one. I have a friend who teaches at a community college, and he is extremely happy there. His main focus is the classroom, of course. But I've known a fair number of younger academics who have landed jobs at places they cannot tolerate, for one reason or another. Often, they hope to teach at a "better" institution, or one where a good deal more research and writing is expected. If you find yourself in these circumstances, remember that it is not impossible to "publish your way out" of wherever you happen to find yourself. There will always be a substantial demand for high-level, productive scholars. If you want to become one of these, you will have to dedicate yourself to the task in rather specific ways, finding the time to engage in research, to attend conferences, to read the journals in your field, and to meet other people engaged in the type of research that interests you. All of this can be done.

The crucial thing I would say to anyone entering the profession of teaching is that you must put a high value on the notion of the community of scholars. The academy is a very special place, and takes many different forms. But everyone within the academic village is, to one degree or another, involved in the pursuit of truth, the acquisition of knowledge. A high premium is placed within this community on the notion of discourse. You will be expected to take positions, to argue for them, and to be willing to change your mind when new information is presented, if that information warrants a changed mind. Be flexible but tough. Be willing to take risks, in your conversations with colleagues and students, in your writing and research. No good will come of shyness, laziness, timidity. Expect the community to support your efforts, and they will: just as you show support for those around you.

This is all simple stuff. I only wish somebody had sent me this letter, and that I had read it, about 30 years ago. It would have made my passage a little easier.

OFFICE HOURS

Wittgenstein had an extraordinary gift for divining the thoughts of the person with whom he was engaged in discussion. While the other struggled to put his thoughts into words, Wittgenstein would . . . state them for him. This power of his, which sometimes seemed uncanny, was made possible, I am sure, by his own prolonged and continuous researches. He knew what someone else was thinking because he had himself travelled innumerable times through those twists and turns of reasoning.

—Noel Malcolm, *Ludwig Wittgenstein: A Memoir*

Office hours punctuate the working life of all professors, a familiar part of academic life. They are usually less intense than the hours spent in front of a class, but many of the best teaching experiences I've had have taken place within those appointed times. Term after term, decade after decade, I've waited with my door slightly ajar, my feet on the desk, open for a very special kind of business.

Part of the fun of office hours is that you never know who will wander in: a student from the past, long forgotten, mired in some midlife crisis or eagerly hoping to reignite his interest in the field; a current student, anxious about an upcoming paper or exam; a friend of a friend, whose daughter or son is a high school student in search of a college; an agitated colleague or one with a joke to share; a publisher's representative, packing the latest textbook in the field like a six-gun. I could extend this list ad infinitum.

A number of unexpected visits to my office stand out in memory. The one I recall most vividly occurred during my first year of teaching at St. Andrews. It was a gray Scottish day in the early seventies, when I had an office on the top floor of Castle House, a granite building with amazing views of the North Sea and a ruined medieval fortress. I was a teaching fellow and known as someone willing to read and discuss student poems. (Creative writing, as a subject, had not yet surfaced in Scottish universities. That would come later, to St. Andrews, with a vengeance, modeled on the American MFA program.) I had set aside a couple of hours on Wednesday afternoons, when by custom there were no classes. I had informal meetings with anybody who had a poem in need of attention. On this particular occasion, a little old woman knocked tentatively, and almost didn't enter when I shouted, "Come in!"

She had a round, weather-beaten face, and wore a long cloth coat and a puffy hat. "Are you the poem man?" she asked, her accent rustling with the peculiar consonantal sounds native to the East Neuk of Fife.

"I'm the one," I said.

She entered the room anxiously and took a seat opposite my desk, shuffling through a vast handbag. "I've written a poem," she said, firmly, producing a text written in a bold script. "It's of a personal nature."

It was a poem of disappointed love, and I remember verbatim the searing final lines:

And memory was the syphilis

Contracted when you screwed me

With electricity and detachment.

I paused to let these lines sink in fully, then raised a cautious eyebrow. "With electricity *and* detachment?" I wondered, gently. She tightened her lips and said, with something like long-repressed rage: "It's *true.*"

I didn't doubt that it was true. I never doubt that the astonishing stories I've heard over the years during my office hours are true. These include tales of hair-raising adventures abroad in remote places, wild rides in strange vehicles, savage family dynamics, tragic losses, misplaced or computer-eaten papers, freak accidents, unrequited loves, and mysterious illnesses. Once in a while, a student actually comes into my office with a question related to a course.

In St. Andrews, the Oxford tutorial system reigned, partly in imitation of Oxford and Cambridge, where many of the faculty had studied. I quickly became addicted to the pleasures and rigors of one-on-one teaching—first as a student, then as a teacher. The system worked like this: a course of formal lectures was delivered in a drafty hall to a large number of drowsing undergraduates. Attendance was never required at these performances, and was usually sketchy. But students were always assigned to tutors, whom they met once a week (individually or in groups of two or three) in the tutor's office. I had some of my best moments, as a student, in these tutorials.

One genial professor in the History Department insisted that students come for weekly tutorials to his house, which was only a short walk from the university's central campus. To say that this house was untidy does not do justice to the shambles of that place: old newspapers and books were piled in precarious towers, while oversized cats prowled the furniture, which had seen better days—perhaps in a previous century. You were invariably served brutally strong tea and stale biscuits by the tutor's long-suffering and forlorn-looking wife, who stood silently near the door of her husband's study, listening to the tutorial and waiting for the student's cup to require a refill. The professor's study was miserably cold, unheated except for a double-barred "electric fire," which was placed close enough to the student's ankles to cause serious burns if you weren't careful. You would read aloud from your assigned essay while the tutor cleaned his pipe, sometimes muttering assent or shaking his head in disbelief. The ritual presentation of the essay was followed by a wry critique. "No, Mr. Parini," he once intoned, "You cannot generalize about the feudal system in the United Kingdom during the Dark Ages. There was no such place as the United Kingdom at that time. Indeed, there were no Dark Ages."

I always liked rueful remarks by my tutors, especially this one, but my own temperament as a teacher disallows sarcasm in dealing with students, though I aspire to a certain frankness when discussing their work, especially during one-on-one encounters. It does not advance a student's intellectual progress to offer lame praise and avoid the problems at hand. Office hours provide a place and time where honest criticism can occur without the social interference that makes the classroom a more complex forum for criticism. I would never purposely embarrass a student in front of his or her peers, but I don't mind saying difficult things when huddled over a paper, a poem, or story in my office.

Teaching, at its best, is personal. It involves the interaction, even the clashing, of separate wills. One can always get mere information from a textbook, so the "passing on" of facts is the least of a teacher's job. Transforming those facts into feelings is the real work of education. It's often a question of attitude, quite literally: where a particular human being stands *in relation to* a body of knowledge, a text, an argument. This kind of relational knowledge can, of course, be transmitted by a good lecture, but it's never easy to know where the students stand during a lecture, what their attitudes toward the material might be. Do they understand what I'm saying? Do they agree or disagree with my subjective judgments? Am I confusing them? Am I boring them? These questions often scurry through my brain while I'm lecturing. During office hours, the student's attitude becomes apparent, and the teacher has the opportunity to adjust that attitude or—wonderfully—to have his or her attitude adjusted by the student.

I find myself challenged, often brought up short, by students again and again. It's part of the work of self-education that goes on as my own opinions undergo revision in the interest of greater understanding, fuller knowledge. Just recently, I found myself upbraided by a young man who had listened in class to my views about the U. S. invasion of Iraq, which I had considered barbarous and foolish, likely to increase American isolation in the world and play directly into the hands of terrorists. I recall saying in my class that I found it particularly galling that critics of the war had had their patriotism challenged by various commentators and politicians, who seemed to have little regard for the operations of democracy—a system of government that depends on the clash of opinion for its very existence. This particular student came into my office looking anxious. He explained that he was from Tennessee, and that his friends and neighbors at home did in fact see things differently. There was a tradition of patriotism in the South that didn't admit much in the way of dissent, especially during times of war. He himself felt that my tone in class was too scathing, and that I was assuming the worst motives in those who found critics of the war unpatriotic. "Perhaps you *are* unpatriotic?" he wondered, with only the slightest edge of irony in his voice.

We spent at least an hour in my office, tossing around the idea of what it meant to be patriotic, and what anti-Americanism was. The student had spent the previous term in Italy, and I wondered if anybody in that country had ever been accused of being "anti-Italian." It seemed unlikely. But the boy stood his ground, and I was left feeling somewhat chastened and apologetic. I live in Vermont, surrounded by liberal-minded colleagues and friends, most of whom regarded the invasion of Iraq as an act of ill-considered belligerence likely to set the wrong sort of precedent and sure to backfire in the long run, increasing the already-strong resentment of American power abroad. That this view represents only one side of a complex argument was brought forcefully before me by this student, and I know that I benefited enormously by having my cherished assumptions challenged. I am more cautious now when I allude to this subject in class.

In one-on-one situations, during office hours, there is often an exchange between teacher and student that can only be called erotic. I think George Steiner puts this well in *Lessons of the Masters*, his little book on teaching: "Eroticism, covert or declared, fantasized or enacted, is interwoven in teaching, in the phenomenology of mastery and discipleship. This elemental fact has been trivialized by a fixation on sexual harassment. But it remains central. How could it be otherwise?" This subject—the erotic transfer between teacher and student, and its pitfalls—has been much on the mind of contemporary writers, from David Mamet and J. M. Coetze to Francine Prose, Saul Bellow, and others. Indeed, the homoerotic tensions between Alcibiades and Socrates, as dramatized in *The Symposium*, represent a classic example. Nobody who has taught for very long has not experienced the strange allure and intimacy of the teacher-student relationship; it goes beyond sex. It moves beyond what psychologists refer to as transference. There is true love in the passing on of knowledge, and this involves understanding: the teacher must really know the student, on some deep level, for teaching of the most intense kind to happen. The student must have real love for the teacher. We have all experienced this, from first grade through graduate school, and beyond. I have loved my best teachers. And this *eros* is naturally dangerous as well as beneficial.

I fully understand the dangers of sexual harassment, and I understand that transference is often involved, in that students will think of the teacher as their father or mother. There is a peculiar power that a teacher exercises over a student, and one of the benefits of experience on the teacher's part is knowing how to use that power to benefit students, not hurt them. The seductive power of good teaching can easily collapse into mere sexual stimulation; that is unfortunate. But this power can be used for good as well as ill, and there is really no possibility of denying this reality. The erotics of teaching must be understood and mastered; they must be *used*.

I often think of an old saw I heard from John Dickey, a former president of Dartmouth, whom I used to meet for drinks occasionally when I first started teaching. He said, "All that an education requires is an interested student, a committed teacher, and a reasonably good log." We have some pretty expensive logs to sit on nowadays, but the formula is still the same: one committed teacher, one interested student, and two chairs in a quiet office. There's almost no way to calculate where you can go from there, but the journey will often be exhilarating—for teacher and student alike.

ON LECTURING

We speak, but it is God who teaches.

—St. Augustine

Despite well-intentioned efforts to limit class sizes at many colleges and universities, the lecture remains in place as a primary teaching format. The economics of higher education are such that few institutions can afford to discard these courses altogether, however much a small seminar is preferred by students and faculty alike. With only one paid teacher and a large roomful of tuition-paying students, how can you beat the numbers? In my view, this is not necessarily a bad thing.

There is a great tradition of lecturing, of course. It goes back to the brotherhood of Pythagoras, the Academy in Athens, and various schools, such as the Peripatetics and the Sophists, who moved from village to village, drawing sizable crowds in private houses or public forums, collecting fees for their disquisitions. (One of them, Prodicus, apparently charged as much as 50 drachmae for a lecture on the proper use of language: an incredible sum in those days.) In the eleventh and twelfth centuries, wandering scholars went from city to city, searching for an audience, often in vain; groups of interested students would band together and hire the good ones. If the scholar's lectures failed to stimulate and instruct, the customers walked away, and the lecturer starved or took up archery or falconry. In such a system, it paid to have your lecturing skills well honed.

In many ways, nothing has changed. Few teachers in American colleges can earn their keep by giving only tutorials or seminars, though anyone knows that the best teaching experiences usually occur in these intimate settings, where minds rub against each other, and where students can test their knowledge of a discipline actively. In an ideal world, small classes and individual tutorials would reign; but even in that world, lectures would be missed. Good lectures, that is.

There is probably nothing more insufferable than a really bad lecture. Everyone who has been to college has sat in one of those miserable seats with the flipped up writing arm, doodling in a notebook (or, too often, on the arm of the desk itself) as the uninspired, deadly prof wastes an hour or more of precious time. I never found those hours completely useless, since daydreaming can be productive, a time for planning social encounters, thinking up future projects, reminiscing. (I have had some of my best erotic thoughts while listening to erudite but boring presentations on various arcane subjects.) Moreover, I love to doodle: making lists of odd words or inventing titles for unwritten poems or novels. As a student, I often amused myself by writing bawdy limericks that in some way involved the lecturer. (There was a professor called X / Who was never much given to sex. . . .) The problem was, I tended to laugh aloud at unexpected, inappropriate times, thereby unsettling the lecturer, making a bad lecture even worse.

I also experienced some intensely creative and stimulating lecturers—the sort who made me eager to find out more about the subject, who made me really understand why they found their discipline important, even thrilling. These lecturers could hold me, and the class, in a spell, as would a good play. In fact, the analogy works well: the lecture hall was a theater, the teacher an actor. One got to observe a person thinking out loud, caught in the act of finding solutions to real problems, engaging the subject as if life itself depended on the results. The lecturer, in these instances, managed to generate suspense, with the class wondering if he or she would pull it off, this magical act, "the mind in the act of finding / what will suffice," as Wallace Stevens once wrote.

One professor in St. Andrews, Lionel Butler, would sweep into a crowded lecture hall in his long, black gown; he insisted that students wear their scarlet gowns: the traditional dress of undergraduates in St. Andrews. These gowns added to the sense of theater. Butler's entrances and exits were wildly dramatic, and the lectures themselves were elegant little historical dramas, crafted to perfection. Professor Butler specialized in the Crusades, and anyone who attended his lectures felt as though they had been to Jerusalem and back by the end of term.

The truth is that great lectures cannot be faked: every student knows this instinctively. This means that every genuinely good lecture is the product of a lifetime's commitment to a body of knowledge, a product of years of thinking and reading; the lecture represents—and presents—a way of being in the world while demonstrating a certain mastery of a discipline. It also represents an unfolding of meaning, a process of Becoming that leads into Being—or what the Greeks called *aletheia*. I was always moved, and still am, when I sit in a large room and listen to someone speaking from the heart without pretense about something that he or she finds essential. Of course it takes considerable skill and real courage to speak, nakedly and forthrightly, with controlled emotion, in front of an audience, especially a young audience. Students can be very dismissive, even contemptuous.

I always wish I had heard Wittgenstein at Cambridge. He

taught well before my time, but I have read many accounts of his performances and talked with several people who actually experienced his famous classes. He always had a specific philosophical problem in mind as he walked into the lecture hall, his face hardened into thought, his eyes expressionless, as though cutting off the sensory world from his brain. He would worry the problem of the day aloud, as if the shutters of his mind—an awesome thing in itself—were flung open, and the class could look into the whirring mechanism of his brain. This was, in his own term, a process of "showing" or "ostentation." This was teaching in its root sense: *techen*, which in Middle English means "demonstrate" or to point in a direction. Wittgenstein was the ideal teacher in many ways, one who showed students what it meant to think. He didn't give them answers; he presented a way, a technique, for finding answers to problems. He also showed them how to formulate a problem, and taught them how to value the act of formulation.

In a sense, he was a Socratic teacher, believing that the solutions to problems were, indeed, inherent. "A person caught in a philosophical confusion," he once said to Noel Malcolm, "is like a man in a room who wants to get out but doesn't know how. He tries the window but it is too high. He tries the chimney but it is too narrow. And if he would only *turn around*, he would see that the door has been open all the time!" His constant belief was that a problem is usually best solved by arranging the material already in the mind's possession, not by seeking and finding new information.

Tone was important to Wittgenstein during a lecture. Malcolm recalls that he would often invent fanciful examples to illustrate a point, and these could strike him as amusing. His face would brighten, and he would "grin at the absurdity of what he imagined." If anyone in the class should grin, however, he would become furious, and shout, "No, no, I'm serious!" "Wittgenstein could not tolerate a facetious tone in his classes," Malcolm writes, "the tone that is characteristic of philosophical discussion among clever people who have no serious purpose." I suspect that the tension generated by the personality of the lecturer, in this case, kept the students alert, on edge, thinking. Again, it was highly theatrical.

Wittgenstein's students sat in his classes rather breathlessly, wondering if so much intellectual effort might actually kill the teacher. He apparently had all the facial and bodily quirks—and intellectual skills—necessary to pull off such an act. He was a real "showman," showing how to solve a problem, and giving students an idea of what a philosophical problem looked like and why he considered it important. His lucky students experienced the *process* of philosophical thinking by sitting at his feet. The good ones often felt they learned how to "do" philosophy by encountering this man in action, this embodiment of what Emerson once called Man Thinking.

Of course one cannot expect every lecturer to behave like Wittgenstein—he was an oddity, idiosyncratic in the extreme, one-off, however marvelous. It would be crazy for a young teacher to emulate him explicitly. Indeed, what every young lecturer must discover is that the style of the lecture must always conform to the style of the teacher's actual personality, reflecting (quite literally) his or her attitude or stance toward the world. There is never much chance of teaching from outside the teacher's natural range of intellect or emotions, or outside the circle of his or her sensibility. Teachers can expand the range of their style; but it will never work to force the issue, as I have myself learned when trying to teach like somebody else. It just doesn't fly. It looks and sounds fraudulent, even ridiculous. And students notice.

If one's natural stance is commonly ironic, for example, irony will pervade the presentation. There will be as many styles of good lecturing as there are individual ways of taking the world and taking oneself, although anyone can learn from the example of Wittgenstein that it helps to convey to students a sense of the process itself, a feeling that what the lecturer is doing has something of the offhand vitality and ad hoc drama of real thought. There is nothing more boring or ineffective than presenting material that has been too firmly codified, hardened into passive knowledge. (I still recall, with dread, a pompous young history professor at my undergraduate college who spent the whole of each lecture presenting the "ten causes of the American Revolution" or the "seven consequences of British taxation on the American colonies." He would solemnly write these on the board, and we were expected to transfer his notes to our notes and repeat these dull sequences on our exams. Not surprisingly, his academic career was blessedly short.)

I am not suggesting that showiness is all. Like everyone who has spent any time in the academic village, I've listened to many flashy lecturers who came off as phony, even slightly ridiculous. Recently I sat through a high-tech performance by a visiting lecturer who came with the works, including a laser pointer that he used to illuminate bullet points on a screen that rolled down from the ceiling at the touch of a button. There were video clips and sound clips as well: everything but belly dancers. The lecture was meticulously organized and obviously well rehearsed. (I can somehow visualize this guy at home in his bathroom, booming his lines before a steamy mirror as he shaves.) For all this, the audience was noticeably bored, even annoyed, by the man's presentation. I certainly was. The problem, I suspect, was that he was faking it. This was a job of work, carefully prepared but uninspired. I never thought for a second that he really cared about what he was saying.

By contrast, I once sat through a course of lectures in St. Andrews by a classicist who had the driest manner on earth. He blew his nose frequently, and spoke with a pronounced lisp. He had a wall-eyed stare that deeply unsettled the audience. His voice was raspy and high pitched. He read from yellowing notes, and his references to current events were at least a decade out of date. Every single aspect of his style was repulsive. Yet he somehow managed to communicate his deep-seated love of the subject, and when he read verses aloud, in Latin, his voice became tremulous. His eyes filled with tears. He seemed to be fighting through his own ridiculous manner to get at something that mattered to him. I always left the lecture hall inspired, eager to get back to my room to reread certain texts and to follow up his suggestions for further reading.

Among the finest lecturers I ever encountered was Isaiah Berlin, whose essays have remained a touchstone of my own emotional and intellectual life. He was, of course, a famously renowned lecturer, someone who held Oxford classes in thrall for six decades, and who lectured around the world to large, grateful audiences. Many years after I attended his lectures as a young man, I would sit with him in his cavernous study at All Soul's College and talk about things that mattered to us both. Once I asked him about his lecturing style, so entirely his own. He spoke way too rapidly, almost comically so. He would boom and sputter away for hours at a time in his deep, bass voice, never pausing, paying no attention to the class whatsoever. His mind worked quickly as he reached for examples, quoting texts in half a dozen languages with the ease of a native speaker. He seemed almost frantic at times, as if the next paragraph—he spoke in perfectly shaped paragraphs—

might well contain the ultimate point about his subject at hand, might even contain the "key to all mythologies," as the Reverend Edward Casaubon in *Middlemarch* would say.

"My lectures are just extensions of my reading, part of my argument with the authors of certain books that I care about," he told me. "I have no method. Like every student in the class, I'm fumbling for the light switch in a very large but very dark room. The students get to watch me fumble." Sir Isaiah was willing, and humble enough, to let the class watch him fumble for that switch.

At this stage in my teaching life, three decades into the profession, I actually love to lecture. I've pretty much given up on detailed lecture notes, preferring a loose outline with key facts in boldface, just to remind me of a date or title or phrase. I have quotations from critics that might come in handy typed out or Xeroxed, for easy access. And I have a text at hand, underlined in bold colors, so that my eye knows readily where to land in the excitement of the moment. Apart from that, I step in front of every class as if naked, glad to be as foolish as necessary to make whatever points I feel I have to make. I only talk about things that matter to me, but I try to explain why these things matter in a way that students can feel what I feel about these things. If all they want are the facts, they can look elsewhere, perhaps in a textbook. But not at me.

CONDUCTING SEMINARS

Anyone who has been privileged to sit through a first-rate seminar understands its value. The seminar is that midpoint between the lecture and the individual tutorial, a place in the curriculum where students get to know the professor in a personal way, and to test their knowledge of a discipline against his or hers. Seminars can be exacting, exhilarating experiences for the teacher and the student alike, although conducting them is difficult work; it requires of the professor a number of skills that can only be acquired through practice and self-discipline.

As college teachers, we usually have no opportunity in graduate school to conduct a seminar. For the most part, we rely on our memory of good seminars to imagine how to lead one ourselves. I had one or two seminars in graduate school that prepared me rather well for thinking about the form itself, and I often talked with my fellow students about what worked and what didn't. It so happened that three of my former teachers or friends had studied at Oxford with the legendary classicist, Eduard Fraenkel, a Berliner of Jewish heritage. In 1934, Fraenkel fled from the Nazis, settling into a chair in classical literature at Corpus Christi College, where he became an instant legend, attracting the best young classicists of the era to his seminars.

"I was terrified in those seminars," Iris Murdoch (who studied with Fraenkel in the late thirties) once said to me. "Fraenkel did not suffer fools gladly." She described his severity—nearly 50 years after the fact—with awe and fascination. Fraenkel had written landmark studies of Plautus and Horace, and he was justly famous for an edition of the *Agamemnon* by Aeschylus that became the standard by which all future editions of classical texts (and commentaries) would be judged. His own commentary was extraordinarily rich and astute, referring to centuries of scholarship with apparent ease, making endless little (but illuminating) judgments along the way: the sort of thing that anyone conducting the Platonic ideal of a seminar might do.

Indeed, Fraenkel reflected on the influence of his Oxford seminars on his later scholarship in his edition of *Agamemnon*: "My favorite reader, whose kindly and patient face would sometimes comfort me during the endless hours of drudgery, looked surprisingly like some of the students who worked with me for many years at Oxford in our happy seminar classes on the *Agamemnon*. Without the inspiring, and often correcting, co-operation of those young men and women I should not have been able to complete the commentary. If they thought a passage to be particularly difficult, that was sufficient reason for me to examine and discuss it as fully as I could; and more than once it was their careful preparation, their inquisitiveness, and their persistent efforts that made it possible to reach what seemed to us like a satisfactory solution." Fraenkel added, a bit later: "Anyone who has conducted seminar classes knows that the common sense of the young often shatters the subtle devices of their elders and that only bad teaching can deter them from speaking their mind."

Fraenkel makes it plain that the success of his seminars depended on two-way criticism: the professor may originate a notion; but students "correct" that notion. There is give-and-take. The seminar itself demands a fluidity, an ease, wherein the pursuit of truth rises above any ego demands on the part of the person conducting the seminar. The seminar itself comes alive in the dialectic, the process of working toward a sense of shared under-standing. Fraenkel put his trust in the students, in their ability to listen, to make fine discriminations, and to apply "the common sense of the young," something that can get lost as one ages.

My old friend Gordon Williams, a well-known Latin scholar from Yale and former student of Fraenkel's, remembered him after his death in an essay. "To Fraenkel, teaching was the communica-tion of scholarship and he was a brilliant teacher," he writes. "Even apathetic students were infected with the vitality of ideas that struck home because they were actually lived by the speaker. In this way he roused interest in subjects like Greek metre which ordinary teachers reduce to mechanical formulae. Metre was for him the sound and movement of poetry and song: recitation (even singing) was predominant in such lectures (his raucous and ponderous rendering of the frog-song in *Frogs* was memorable). But his greatest contribution to teaching at Oxford was made in seminars, at least one of which he held every year almost to the very day of his death. . . . These seminars were occasions of formidable and immediate confrontations with a very great scholar and, as such, terrifying. A victim once laughingly described the scene as a circle of rabbits addressed by a stoat. But most students learnt to forget terror in the sheer interest of learning to express their ideas and of having them tested against Fraenkel's scholarship and in applying some of his techniques themselves."

Needless to say, few leaders of seminars can hope to match Fraenkel, but one can learn a good deal by listening to accounts of such a teacher. When I began teaching, at Dartmouth in the midseventies, I was handed a seminar in my first year. I chose the topic: "The Artist and Society." We read books by James Joyce, Jean-Paul Sartre, Thomas Mann, and others. I still recall the polished table in a room over Baker Library. A dozen eager and highly intelligent students huddled around it. The main impression I have from that seminar is hearing the sound of my own voice. I was frightened, and I talked way too much. When students talked, I was too busy thinking up my responses to hear what they were saying in a deep way. It would not surprise me if they all found the seminar very boring.

"I sat in dread," Iris Murdoch said to me, "waiting for Fraenkel's eyes to swivel in my direction. 'Miss Murdoch,' he would say, 'what do you make of these lines?'" I doubt that anyone has ever sat in dread in my seminars, and I'm rather glad for that. The old Germanic version of the professor as master of the universe, as a commanding figure who terrifies students and will not suffer insufficiently brilliant responses, does not wash in the democratic world of American colleges. Nevertheless, students do not require a dominating and erudite figure to feel intimidated. It's frightening enough to have to say something, anything, around a seminar table, in front of your peers, no matter what the professor's bearing.

I have learned, over the years, to listen more attentively when students speak, and to take what they say—even the "foolish" things—seriously. (The best teachers can pan gold in unlikely waters.) Paying attention does not mean simply turning your eyes in the student's direction, focusing somewhere above the bridge of the nose. It means gauging the attitude of students toward the material, assessing the level of their understanding, trying to figure out *how* as well as *what* they think about a particular topic. It means refusing to respond too quickly, or perfunctorily, just to keep the conversation flowing.

It seems useful to recall that one "conducts" a seminar. The analogy with a musical conductor is appropriate and instructive. The subject of the seminar (and the texts or problems being considered) forms a kind of score; the students will already have, with greater or lesser degrees of success, mastered the score before coming to class. The expectation is, in fact, that they will have prepared for class by reading the material, by thinking up something to say. The work of the conductor is to draw out this intellectual music, to arrange it, set the tempo of play. Imagine an orchestra, if you will, *without* a conductor. There would be no pace, no emphasis, no interpretation. A group of students meeting to discuss, say, *Hamlet*, without a seminar leader, would meander and digress. There would be no teasing out of Hamlet's motives, or the motives of his mother and her husband. There might well be no highlighting of important themes, motifs, symbolic patterns. Significant passages could easily be glossed over.

A seminar invariably reflects the personality of the professor, the one who "conducts" the class, creating the mood, setting the conversation in motion and shaping its course. I take this for granted. But a good seminar will also reflect the personality of the students. I begin every seminar these days with this preface: "This seminar is not about me. It's about you. The success or failure of the class will rest on your shoulders as well as mine. We must pull together, participating as fully as possible, sharing our thoughts and feelings about this material, listening to each other respectfully and closely. The only thing I expect of you when you walk into this room is, well, everything. I want your heart and mind at this table."

Over the years, I've learned how to pace a seminar. It is always useful to have one or two vivid questions in mind for the class to "answer" in the course of each session, and students should be given these in advance. I often end a class by saying: "Next time, we'll be thinking about X. Why is it that this or that is so? How can we be sure?" Students should have specific assignments, and certain ones should be responsible on a given day for responding to a text or question. This is the basic architecture of the seminar— the essential score, if you will. The work of the seminar leader is "conducting" the class through the allotted time, drawing all—or most—students into discussion, cutting off digressions when they seem unrelated to the main line of argument, questioning students when they say things that are either unclear or perhaps unfounded.

A great scholar like Fraenkel was, I suspect, rarely mistaken about the meaning of a passage, although even he was open to being "corrected," as he said. He apparently enjoyed these moments of enlightenment. For my part, I'm quite often wrong about things, and expect students to "correct" me frequently. I put the notion forward that we must all risk making statements, based on hunches; we must then test those statements against the text, against the forces of reason. In doing so, we will have to revise our formulations. The work of the group, in fact, is to refine these formulations, to move steadily toward greater understanding, more accurate statements.

One gradually, as a teacher, comes to appreciate group dynamics. Frequently students come to class unprepared. In this situation, I avoid shaming them as a matter of principle, but I'm not against making them feel the burden of their inaction. "John, I see that you haven't read 'The Oven Bird' very closely," I might say. "Otherwise, you could not imagine it is a poem about a Thanksgiving turkey." Humor, as ever, makes criticism more palatable. I have rarely found students willing to come to class and be chided over and over again about their lack of preparation. I will often give them a special assignment for the next session; they will "lead us off," I always say. This puts them on the spot, and usually gets them involved.

Students come alive in a seminar when they find themselves talking and making judgments that their peers, and their professor, find sensible or interesting. It's always possible to discover one's students' level of understanding, and to lead them forward as they begin to make new connections, begin to "find" themselves as thoughtful people who can express and question ideas that are raised by the professor or by other students around the table. Half the work of any seminar—from the professor's viewpoint—is getting students involved in a serious way.

There is no substitute for preparation, as everyone who has ever led a seminar must realize. The teacher must have a deep and passionate knowledge of the material, being aware of the relevant scholarship and competing approaches to the subject. He or she must be willing to make this complex knowledge available to students, and to model critical thinking at every moment. This can be intimidating to students; but it's worth it. Students should come away from a seminar understanding that the professor has genuinely been moved by the material, and that certain standards—certain *values*—are involved in making judgments. I like to be very frank and honest, explain to my students why certain poems, for example, have been crucial in my emotional as well as intellectual development as a person, as a member of the community of scholars. I like it when the seminar itself models that community, becomes a room full of excited conversation, debate, good humor, rigorous thinking, and—of course—*learning*.

THE RESPONSIBILITY OF THE TEACHERS

College teachers, as members of that often-suspect group known as intellectuals, have a huge responsibility, to society and to their students. In his seminal essay, "The Responsibility of Intellectuals," Noam Chomsky meditates on the role of intellectuals in society, underlining their obligations: "Intellectuals are in a position to expose the lies of government, to analyze actions according to their causes and motives and often hidden intentions. In the Western world, at least, they have the power that comes from political liberty, from access to information and freedom of expression." Those living and working within the academy have the leisure time, the information resources, and the analytical skills required to mount a sustained critique of public deception by governments and corporations. Few of them will, of course, take the trouble to exercise their power in this regard, and that is unfortunate; but the classroom is another matter.

The notion of "politicizing" the classroom horrifies many, with good reason. For the most part, societies have made sure that schools and universities are places where the young are trained to perform in ways that promote the interests of the status quo. As James Bryant Conant, a former Harvard president and philosopher of education noted many years ago in *The Child, the Parent, and the State*: "Some teachers and administrators object at once to any line of argument which starts with such phrases as 'the nation needs today.' Their attention has been centered for so long on the unfolding of the individuality of each child that they automatically resist any idea that a new national concern might be an important factor in planning a program." Conant argued that schools and colleges must work hard to train "scientists" who could fight the Cold War and to provide a managerial class for American corporations. God forbid that a teacher should ignore "national goals" when teaching a class.

In many countries, such as Italy and France, professors are direct employees of the state. Indeed, this is true of most state universities in the United States. It therefore seems almost beside the point that teachers should pursue anything like a critique of their own government or society from within the academy. "Objectivity" means criticizing other states, other forms of government. (Thus, during the Cold War, nobody would have seemed "out of line" to judge Communist China, Cuba, or the Soviet Union harshly. That would have been perfectly acceptable, even expected. After the sixties, of course, one has seen a number of Marxist critics on American campuses—a group much attacked by the right, who imagine some kind of infiltration of subversives. In the first years of the twenty-first century, it would be difficult to find anyone in a professional department of government boasting an allegiance to Marxist doctrine. Marxist oddballs tend to cluster in language and literature departments, where the jargon is so thick that nobody can understand what they are saying anyway, rendering them harmless.

The traditional assumption on American campuses is that professors will teach in an ideologically neutral fashion, therefore "objectively." But simply to ignore politics is neither good teaching nor good moral sense. In literature courses, for example, I often deal with poets and novelists who express strong political opinions in their writing; there is no way around this, unless one meticulously churns through the literature to censor those who offend the doctrine of neutrality. To do this would be to bowdlerize the material in ways that are "political" in the worst way. I suspect it would be difficult to find *any* subject in the humanities where politics does not impinge, explicitly as well as implicitly. Not to acknowledge this impingement is to court irresponsibility as a teacher and serious intellectual.

I hesitate even to use the word "intellectual" at all. There is such rampant anti-intellectualism in America that we almost forget that the term appropriately describes a function. Intellectuals work with their minds, framing and manipulating concepts and ideas. Teachers are, by definition, intellectuals, in that they not only work with their own minds, but demonstrate to generations of young people how they can work with theirs, assimilating information, sorting information, making judgments about the validity and proportion of constructs. The problem is that the term has negative implications.

The term carries with it (historically) a sense of opposition. It dates back to the nineteenth century, and came into play during the infamous Dreyfus Affair, when "intellectuals" such as Émile Zola took an unpopular stand against their government, which had unfairly accused a man of spying. The right-wing press—and most of the press in France in the late nineteenth century fit this description—railed against "intellectuals," who seemed not to understand that their function was to support the state. Intellectuals—writers, journalists, teachers—usually did. In Russia, of course, any number of revolutionary types saw themselves as "intellectuals," and they instigated a revolution. In the United States in the early twentieth century, bohemian intellectuals flooded the cities, causing trouble. Even in England there were wise-ass brainy types, such as the Fabians. Bernard Shaw and Bertrand Russell were writers, and they were troublemakers. (Russell was tossed into jail for opposing the First World War.) At least that is how the establishment regarded them.

During the fifties, the Civil Rights Movement brought into play a number of intellectuals, although the term hardly applies to Martin Luther King or Jesse Jackson, noble as they have been. During the Vietnam War, a small group of intellectual activists got to work, helping to frame opposition to the war. A large popular movement began with a few persistent thinkers on campuses. Feminist intellectuals followed in the seventies, effecting substantial changes in society. And there has been a steady trickle of social activists on campuses for the past 30 years: feminists, environmentalists, war resisters, campaigners for civil rights and liberties. For the most part, there is very little sense of the intellectual as critic here. How often do any of those included in the above categories actually take a stand in opposition to the majority opinion, or "out of line" with the ruling viewpoint? Occasionally, as in the late sixties, a small group of intellectuals succeeded in shifting public opinion, as in the case of Vietnam. But this was exceptional.

For the most part, intellectuals continue to work to keep the system afloat, even to discourage active questioning of basic assumptions. During the recent war on Iraq, for example, a large community of political analysts (often drawn from college faculties or so-called Think Tanks) collaborated with the government to persuade a gullible public that Saddam Hussein posed a direct threat to American security. Night after night on public television and various cable channels, experts assembled (with a few notable exceptions) to warn of Weapons of Mass Destruction. This threat, as we discovered, was wildly exaggerated, although many of these same "intellectuals"—such as Kenneth M. Pollack—rushed in with further arguments to justify the war: Saddam was a bad person, who had to be eradicated, he was a force of destabilization in the Middle East; he had killed his own people. And so forth.

The real and obvious questions were largely ignored. Why eliminate Saddam and not one of several dozen *other* dictators around the world who exploit or persecute their own people? Why did the intellectual establishment allow the Bush administration to get away with making Saddam and Osama bin Laden seem equivalent, when they were clearly on either side of a religious and political divide? How could the government get away with failing to plan for the aftermath of war? Why did we *really* invade Iraq? Was it for oil, as most people in the world (outside of U. S. borders) simply assume? Where was the hard-nosed, skeptical analysis we deserved?

American *motives* are rarely questioned by intellectuals in the service of state power. Just spend a profitless Sunday morning watching the talk shows, where "intellectuals" gather to discuss the week's news. It is blithely and uncritically assumed that the American government acts in ways that reflect the majority wishes of tax payers, in the best interests of people at home and abroad, with generosity of spirit and a warm, good heart. The truth is, of course, that American governments have traditionally acted like all powerful governments: to further the interests, economic and social, of those who have paid to elevate them into positions of power. Especially (but not only) in democratic societies, this means that governments must insure the cooperation of the masses. Intellectuals, in this scenario, play a crucial role in making sure that the wrong questions are asked, the hard questions avoided.

This sounds awfully cynical, and I do want to avoid running the usual line here. Many intelligent and honest people work seriously to provide sensible and humane critiques of American power. In the academy, there has been a good deal of "deconstruction," although one cannot help but notice the almost comical ineffectuality of this activity. If, as many popular critics of the academy charge, there has been a pervasive "liberal" attempt—on campuses, in the media—to identify class interests, to uncover racial and ethnic prejudice, and to promote the causes of the underprivileged, the current situation suggests that these efforts have been rather lame. In fact, few students leaving college nowadays have actually been "radicalized" by their professors. If anything, the latest crop of graduates seems apolitical, largely concerned with their own economic survival.

The media, as ever, provide distraction. There is so much "entertainment" about that everyone is perpetually preoccupied, playing the emotional and intellectual equivalent of video games. I rarely see a young person on an airplane or train who is not attached to a device for piping music into his or her ears. The television is now awash with channels, all purveying the same fare: sporting events, music videos, lame comedy programs centered on young men and women who want to have fun at the expense of everyone else in the world, "reality" programs that have nothing to do with reality, cheap action movies, and talk shows where nobody has anything serious to say. Social criticism does manage to creep into certain cartoon shows, such as *The Simpsons* or *South Park*, although this criticism is safely deflected, masked as cynicism. For the most part, one could watch a million hours of television a year without stumbling onto a serious critical thought.

One of the few places in a young person's life where the possibility of serious criticism exists remains the college class-room. I remember going to college in 1966 as a naïve freshman who still retained many assumptions about the nature of the universe that had been taught to me in a fundamentalist Baptist church, which I was forced to attend for much of my young life. During my first semester, I took an introductory course in religion; we read the work of modern theologians like Paul Tillich, Rudolph Otto, and Reinhold Niehbur. I was stunned: disoriented, upset, even angry. My professor, a jovial man who nevertheless made it clear that he was highly skeptical of all religious dogma, understood my crisis of faith, and I spent hours in his office, running through the usual arguments for and against the authority of the Bible, the existence of God, the nature of Christian values. My interior world was overturned, permanently. I became aware of sophisticated theological and philosophical arguments that had, of course, been in play in the community of scholars for more than a century, going back to the German Higher Criticism. Having taken that course, I would never be the same again.

I wish more students coming to college would find their values challenged, even overturned. Everything in a student's previous life has been geared toward conformity and the acceptance of societal values. Blind allegiance to the flag, to some religious dogma, to a team, to a given social class, are implicitly taught by the media, by coaches and parents, by church and school administrators. There are always a high-school teacher or two who manage to sow a few seeds of doubt in receptive students, but genuinely critical thinking is scarce on the ground. The college experience thus becomes a crucial space where education in its most meaningful form can occur.

I try to speak as openly as possible about my political feelings in class, making it clear that these are *my* feelings, and not God's truth. Students need to know that their teacher lives in the world, is affected by ideas, by public events. I often say that I want my students, by implication, to learn to read the world as well as certain canonical texts. This means paying attention to public discourse, and seeing the relationship between what is said on the news, talked about in public, and what poets and novelists choose to say—and how they say it.

It is often revealing to take a segment from a speech by a political leader, such as the president, and subject it to the kind of scrutiny one usually reserves for a poem. Political language, more than ever, has become a Trojan horse; the language looks innocent enough, and seems to say something. But packed inside, hidden, are the explosives. When President Bush says explicitly that "our aim in Iraq is peace," we had better reach for our rifles.

As Chomsky notes, intellectuals—and teachers—are in a position to unmask lies, to reason in public, to ask questions that will rarely get asked in the media. I certainly found the classroom a thrilling place as a student during the Vietnam War because so many of my teachers accepted their responsibility, and refused to go along with public deception. My teachers challenged me to reconsider a whole range of notions about the nature of reality that I took for granted as God's truth. I am still grateful to them for their efforts on my behalf, and I want to act in my own classroom in ways that do justice to their example.

Endings

It's spring in the academic village, with blossoming fruit trees all over campus, the ground smelling of fresh mud, and once again my thoughts turn to summer. I think of those long, delicious months when, without the telephone ringing and student papers sitting on my desk ungraded, without faculty meetings and office hours, without classes to prepare, I'm free again to work exclusively on my own writing. My e-mails will dwindle to communications with a few good friends. Some mornings, I might even sleep in.

But spring also brings with it a small feeling of dread. "April is the cruelest month," wrote T. S. Eliot—a memorable line. I think of it again as lawn mowers drone outside the open windows of my classroom, a sweet wind blows papers off my desk, and I begin to anticipate the end of another school year, with the many losses that inevitably attend that moment, marked so vividly by the graduation ceremony, when half a dozen kids I had really come to like, even love, wave to me from the platform as they proceed into their adult life, diplomas in hand. I'm aware that one or two from each class will remain friends forever, but I know as well that there will be many—

the majority of those whom I genuinely considered friends—who won't. It's not their fault, I tell myself. They will get busy. Soon spouses and children will lay claim to their attention. I'm just a passing figure in their lives; they know this, and I know it. It's not as bad as it sounds, given the demands I feel myself toward spouse and family, toward a circle of friends that has widened decade by decade. There is only so much attention to go around.

I begin to feel this little dread coming on in late March, when the spring snows in Vermont begin to thaw. Huge piles of the stuff grow wet at the edges, melting slowly, so that by the middle of April there are puddles everywhere, and I have for the first time to wear my waders to school. It's called mud season in Vermont, and it brings with it a certain sloppiness of feeling as well. I start to anticipate wrapping things up in each course, turning over in my head potential exam questions and topics for final papers. I make frantic phone calls to students working on senior projects, reminding them that their revisions are almost due, and that the end is near. It's at this point that I begin to mark the seniors as people who will soon pass from my life, probably forever.

The situation this year is, perhaps, exacerbated by the so-called empty nest syndrome. The second of my three sons will leave high school at the end of this term. He has been accepted at the college he really wants to attend, so I guess he's really going. He's going somewhere I can't follow—and would not want to follow. His bedroom will become a guest room, and he will become an honored visitor, a weekender, a person seen at holidays or during term breaks. Our conversations in the years ahead will take place mostly on the telephone. It's called life, and I just don't like many things about it, although I did take solace in a comment in the papers last week by a woman who had just turned 100. When asked if she had any words for somebody who wanted to live to her ripe age, she said, quite simply: "Welcome change."

It's never easy to welcome change. It goes against human nature on some basic level, but I have been vaguely prepared for this pivotal time of life, I suppose, by the loss of favorite students, year after year, for nearly three decades. I've never felt good about their leaving. You meet them as freshmen, with their innocent gazes and acne-blotched skin; they look like high-school kids, and their eagerness during the first few weeks of class is always touching. Soon enough, they become old hands, learning the shortcuts to a good paper, learning how to skim, and so forth. They acquire boyfriends and girlfriends, and their confidence seems to swell. This is gratifying, but there is some loss as well. It can be difficult to regain their attention.

In the spring of their senior year, many students become vulnerable again. I spend hours talking to them in my office, or at home over a cup of tea, about their futures. Should they go into publishing? Can they earn a living as a writer? Is it possible to write on the side and work a job like, say, investment banking? I've become an old hand at answering the routine questions frankly, giving out encouragement without creating a false sense of security. It's not easy to find a job you will like, I tell them; but such jobs do exist. Be adventurous. Follow your bliss, as Joseph Campbell put it. But don't go bankrupt in the process. Always keep alternative job careers in mind. Don't be fussy. If location means a lot to you, start there. And so forth. Everyone who has taught in a college knows the drill.

It is not, of course, only the seniors who will disappear from my life come May or June. Jobs in the academy have been uncertain for three decades. This means that many assistant professors and instructors remain as colleagues for only a year or two. These so-called terminal positions (a hideous term) make for awkward relationships. I grow fond of many younger colleagues. We become friends, share ideas and stories, play basketball or tennis together, eat lunch or dinner at the same table. And then they are gone. It's hard on them, of course, but hard on me, too. Our community is disrupted, and good colleagues are never really "replaced," as the jargon suggests they might be.

The failed tenure cases are perhaps the hardest to bear. Every year, a number of colleagues at Middlebury do not make it through the process. They are given a "terminal year." It's a gruesome prospect. I have been there myself, as we say, having been denied tenure at the first college where I taught. This happened over 20-odd years ago, but I remember vividly the sense of terror I felt. I spent a year walking around the English Department like a ghost, aware that colleagues were afraid to catch my eye. I had no confidence that my career in teaching would continue, and I felt demoralized in the classroom. It was perhaps the worst year of my life, professionally. (The great consolation in my life at this time was that I'd recently gotten married, and was happy as could be in that.)

In the end, I survived the experience rather nicely, and I suspect that my personal history in this regard has made it easier to talk to colleagues who have been "denied," as we say. Though I know it provides only limited comfort, I tell them about my experience, and the experiences of good friends who were denied tenure in earlier years. They often go on to happier lives elsewhere. I certainly did.

Another form of loss comes in the shape of retirements. I am just old enough to have seen more than one generation of older colleagues retire. My experience has been that once these people are gone, you don't see them much. You might run into them in the library, in a dentist's waiting room, or at the post office. They will smile wanly and nod in your direction, as if to say: "Do you still recognize me?" You recognize them perfectly well, even through a mask of age: the deepened wrinkles, the stoop, the whitened hair. At least their voices never change, and there is some comfort in that.

I often dislike the moment at graduation each year when the president asks those retiring from the faculty to stand for a round of applause. It always shocks me when I discover that so-and-so is leaving. How could they? Are they really 60? Sixty-two? Sixty-five? (Of course I'm quite relieved when certain colleagues retire, just as I'm relieved when certain students walk out of my life, diploma in hand. Endings can have a large upside as well.) The retirement of colleagues naturally brings to mind my own retirement. I'm now 56, so I figure I have anywhere from six to nine years of active teaching ahead of me, though it seems impossible to predict the course of one's health or, for that matter, one's feelings as the end approaches. To retire or not to retire, that is the question.

There is always death, too, which seems to hover rather menacingly at the end of every school year, a dark presence behind the mild blue skies. I've never understood why this should be the case, except that parties occur more frequently during the last month or so of spring term, and alcohol flows copiously at these events. Two or three times I've experienced the absolute loss of a student I knew well toward the end of his or her college career, and a certain ominous feeling overcomes me in May.

Endings are gloomy, and one cannot avoid this truth, even while looking for the brighter side. "In my end is my beginning," Eliot also wrote, paraphrasing a French proverb in *Four Quartets*. Indeed, one is reminded again and again by graduation speakers about the root meaning of commencement. Okay, we get it. Students are going out into life, making a transition. This is certainly true, and would anyone prefer it otherwise? I'm even (dimly) aware that I really do want my lovely son to graduate from high school and move on to college. I want him to have a great life, on his own: a free and independent person. For him, I've done the lion's share of my fathering bit, though I'm sure there will be plenty more to come.

Even with students, I'm aware that my role in their lives is often not over. The number of them who stay in touch after graduation always surprises me. For quite a few years, many will require letters of recommendation and career advice. As a creative writing teacher, I expect to see poems and novels in draft for a long time after an especially gifted student has formally left my tutelage. In some happy cases, I find their published books in my mailbox, and it's thrilling. I also know that each year a number of them will return on alumni weekends and look me up, sometimes with a 17-year-old child in tow who wants a tour of the college. Very occasionally, I encounter a former student in the streets of Manhattan or Boston, though sometimes I don't recognize them in business attire, having gotten used to their unisexual sweatshirts, jeans, and sneakers. There is a little comfort in the fact that a handful of former students become friends forever, staying in regular touch.

Walking away from graduation, which always seems to occur on the muggiest day of the year, I experience that grand old thing:

mixed emotions. I'm certainly glad that my seniors made it, that they are going into the world. Their happiness is evident as family and loved ones surround them, kissing them on the forehead and patting their backs. I'm suddenly just an appendage, an interloper, without a function in their lives. They may see me blinking at the periphery, then introduce me to their grandparents and parents, lovers and siblings. "This is Professor Parini," they say, awkwardly. "He was my advisor." Hands are shaken, and I withdraw. They have more on their mind than my feelings, and I have things to do myself. The summer beckons, and I'm suddenly desperate for it to begin.